Criminal Investigation
for the
Professional Investigator

Criminal Investigation
for the
Professional Investigator

Warren J. Sonne

Taylor & Francis
Taylor & Francis Group

Boca Raton   London   New York

A CRC title, part of the Taylor & Francis imprint, a member of the
Taylor & Francis Group, the academic division of T&F Informa plc.

Published in 2006 by
CRC Press
Taylor & Francis Group
6000 Broken Sound Parkway NW, Suite 300
Boca Raton, FL 33487-2742

International Standard Book Number-10: 0-8493-8051-0 (Hardcover)
International Standard Book Number-13: 978-0-8493-8051-8 (Hardcover)
Library of Congress Card Number 2005021173

Library of Congress Cataloging-in-Publication Data

Sonne, Warren J., 1949-
   Criminal investigation for the professional investigator / Warren J. Sonne.
      p. cm.
   ISBN-13: 978-0-8493-8051-8
   ISBN-10: 0-8493-8051-0 (alk. paper)
   1. Criminal investigation--United States. I. Title.

HV8073.S626 2006
363.25'0973--dc22
                                                  2005021173

Taylor & Francis Group
is the Academic Division of Informa plc.

Visit the Taylor & Francis Web site at
http://www.taylorandfrancis.com

and the CRC Press Web site at
http://www.crcpress.com

To Beckie

It's been a long and happy journey.

Preface

DEFINITION

Investigate:

> Function: verb
>
> Inflected Form(s): -gat·ed; -gat·ing
>
> Etymology: Latin *investigatus*, past participle of *investigare* to track, *investigate*, from in- + vestigium footprint, track
>
> *transitive senses*: to observe or study by close examination and systematic inquiry*
>
> *intransitive senses*: to make a systematic examination; especially : to conduct an official inquiry
>
> Synonyms: bug, buzz, candle, case, check out, check over, check up, consider, delve, dig, double O, examine, explore, eyeball, feel out, frisk, go into, inquire, inquisite, inspect, interrogate, listen in, look into, look over, look-see, make inquiry, muckrake, nose around, poke, probe, prospect, pry, question, read, reconnoiter, research, review, run down, scout, scrutinize, search, sift, slurp, spy, stake out, study, tap, wiretap. **

What does it really mean to make "a systematic examination?" Where does one start to learn, or go to hone one's skills within this profession? A daunting task considering the many and varied specialties that are hidden away within the term "investigator." I suppose that the willing candidate could pursue a degree in criminal justice. But wait ... does this advanced education really provide any useful or practical information on investigations? Certainly, learning about the court systems, treatment of juveniles, the mentally ill, and recidivism rates will not hurt, but investigations? No. Perhaps then, the candidate should pursue a Bachelor's and J.D. and then apply to the FBI Academy. Certainly the FBI can teach everyone what he or she needs to know about investigations, right? Close, but no! How about joining

* Merriam-Webster's Online Dictionary, 10th Edition
** Roget's New Millennium™ Thesaurus, First Edition (v 1.1.1) Copyright © 2005 by Lexico Publishing Group, LLC. All rights reserved.

the NYPD? Becoming a fire marshal? Insurance SIU investigator? Computer forensics expert? Private investigator?

Obviously, there is no one right way to become a professional investigator, nor is it possible for any one person to become expert in all of the diverse fields that comprise the investigative community. Yet make no mistake, the field of investigations is a profession and not a trade. To continue upon this path, all investigators need to continually seek self-improvement through basic and advanced training to master their particular specialty. It is equally important that you think of yourself as a professional and to portray that persona to others by looking, speaking, and dressing neatly and appropriately. Professional investigators do not jump to conclusions; rather, they pursue and confirm facts. Professional investigators are dogged in their determination and do not take short cuts. We adhere to codes of ethical and moral behavior that exceed those of society at-large; provide justice to victims; protect the innocent; and provided ourselves with armor against claims of corruption or impropriety.

I write this book based upon my own experiences as a criminal investigative professional with the New York City Police Department, having entered the Narcotics Division in 1972 and retired as a homicide investigator in 1989. My experiences at the NYPD included assignment to investigate organized crime, terrorism, sex crimes, polygraphs, frauds, burglaries, robberies, assaults, deaths, and homicides. I am truly thankful for the extensive training provided to me directly or paid for by NYPD during my career, as well as to the many highly skilled detectives who gladly guided me throughout my career.

Yet, like me, many other professional investigators find that their careers go through a metamorphosis. One day working for the CIA, the next for a civilian competitive intelligence firm. FBI agents may become fraud investigators for credit card companies. Police detectives may become private detectives, and so on. Since retiring from the NYPD, I have founded two private investigation companies; Pinnacle Protective Services, Inc. in New York (www.THENYPI.com), and Sun State Investigative Services, Inc., in Florida (www.THEFLPI.com). It is from that perspective that I am currently working on the second book in the Professional Investigator Series, "Civil Investigations for the Professional Investigator."

The "Professional Investigator" series is being written with the intention of providing all present and future members of the investigative community with the knowledge and insight to motivate them to reach the pinnacle of their respective professions, be it criminal or civil. The series will also provide a bridge to assist those investigators who intend to cross over from one to the other.

For those of you who are reading this book for academic, professional, or personal reasons, I urge you to continue your pursuit to attain the highest professional standing within this noble profession. We are the finders of the facts upon whose work the truth can be found.

Warren J. Sonne

Author

Warren J. Sonne was born in Brooklyn, New York, in 1949 and attended George W. Wingate High School, John Jay College, and the New York Institute of Technology. After high school, Warren joined the New York Police Department (NYPD) as a "police trainee," a pilot project that allowed 18-year-olds to take the police officer's examination and, if successful, to attend the police academy and then be assigned to clerical and administrative positions formerly held by uniformed members.

For the next $2^1/_2$ years Warren worked the telephone switchboards at the 19th Precinct on New York's upper east side and at the 80th Precinct in the Bedford Stuyvesant section of Brooklyn. On his 21st birthday, Warren was appointed as a police officer and assigned to the Special Events Squad, a tactical unit formed to assist with the celebration of the 25th anniversary of the United Nations. Warren left the uniformed service in 1972 when he was assigned to the Narcotics Division, where he worked as both an undercover investigator and a field investigator. For the next 18 years Warren honed his investigative skills, leaving the Narcotics Division in 1976 for the Arson Explosion Division, the predecessor of the now-famous Joint Terrorist Task Force, where he conducted investigations of the FALN, Weather Underground, JDL, Omega 7, and other terrorist groups responsible for bombings in New York City. For the remainder of his career, Warren was assigned to the Queens Sex Crimes Squad, the Queens Task Force, the 108th and 110th Precinct Detective Units, and the Special Investigations Division as a polygraph examiner before finally returning to the 108th Precinct, where he finished his career investigating homicides and developing their intelligence file on Korean gangs. Warren was the recipient of the department's Combat Cross, the NYPD's second highest award "granted to members of the service who, having received honorable mention awards, successfully and intelligently perform an act of extraordinary heroism while engaged in personal combat with an armed adversary under circumstances of imminent personal hazard to life," and numerous other medals. Warren is a member of the NYPD's Honor Legion.

During his NYPD career Warren underwent extensive specialized training, including criminal investigators courses, advanced narcotics training, a Nikon forensic photography course, an arson investigators course, a homicide investigators course, a sex crimes investigators course, explosives investigation training, heavy and automatic weapons training, and a pursuit driving course. Since retiring from the NYPD in 1989, Warren has founded and remains president of two private investigation agencies: Pinnacle Protective Services, Inc., which is licensed and operates in New York, and Sun State Investigative Services, in Florida. Warren's client list includes such high-profile companies as Mercedes Benz, Ford, Freightliner, and GE as well as some of the country's most prestigious law firms. Warren is also the associate editor — law enforcement at *PI Magazine*. Warren has been married to his wife, Rebecca, for 34 years and has two children, Melissa, a practicing attorney in Fort Lauderdale, and Evan, a high school teacher in the Bronx. An avid golfer, Warren now lives in Florida.

CRIMINAL INVESTIGATION (CRI)
INTRODUCTION

In searching for the definitive meaning of the word "crime" I discovered many fanciful explanations, some philosophical, some esoteric, and some that were very practical. Yet it occurred to me that at its foundation we all recognize the basic meaning of "crime" to be the breaking of a law. Western societies have taken great pains to create rules of law, and to devise mechanisms to enforce them. In the CRI Track we will explore one of these mechanisms: criminal investigations.

The FBI has been charged with the task of computing and reporting on crimes committed in the United States since 1930, and they have created a reporting format that classifies crimes into two basic categories: 1) Violent Crimes such as murder, forcible rape, robbery, and aggravated assaults, and 2) the property crimes of burglary, larceny-theft, motor vehicle thefts, and arsons.

This Uniform Crime Reporting (UCR) Program is excellent in providing an insight into crime trends. For example, the UCR release on May 24, 2004, indicates that "the number of violent crimes reported to law enforcement agencies throughout the United States decreased 3.2 percent when compared to figures reported the previous year,"* yet it does not account for all of the crimes committed in the United States. The UCR categories do not report the trafficking in narcotics, or firearms, nor are they concerned with prostitution, gambling, statutory rapes, DWIs, or a multitude of other crimes that are regulated by local, state, or federal laws.

* FBI, Uniform Crime Reports, January-December 2004

Table of Contents

Crime Clearance

1

The Uniform Crime Reporting (UCR) Program also standardizes the acceptable methods that are to be used by police departments for clearing or closing criminal investigations.

1.1 Clearance by Arrest

An offense is "cleared by arrest," or solved for crime-reporting purposes when at least one person is (1) arrested or (2) charged with the commission of the offense and turned over to the court for prosecution (whether following arrest, court summons, or police notice). Although no physical arrest is made, a clearance by arrest can be claimed when the offender is a person under 18 years of age and is cited to appear in juvenile court or before other juvenile authorities.

Several crimes may be cleared by the arrest of one person, or the arrest of many persons may clear only one crime. Further, if several persons are involved in the commission of a crime and only one is arrested and charged, the crime is listed on the Return A as cleared by arrest. When the other persons involved in the crime are arrested at a later date, no record will be made of a clearance by arrest since the offense was already cleared following the arrest of the first person.[*]

1.2 Exceptional Clearance

In certain situations, law enforcement is not able to follow the steps outlined under "clearance by arrest" to clear offenses known to them, even though all leads have been exhausted and everything

---

[*] *UCR Handbook,* pp. 41–42.

possible has been done to obtain a clearance. For crime-reporting purposes, if all of the following questions can be answered affirmatively, then the offense can be cleared "exceptionally."

> 1. Has the investigation definitely established the identity of the offender?
> 2. Is there enough information to support an arrest, charge, and turning over to the court for prosecution?
> 3. Is the exact location of the offender known so that the subject could be taken into custody now?
> 4. Is there some reason outside law enforcement control that precludes arresting, charging, and prosecuting the offender?*

If the answers to the first three questions are yes, some reasons that would fulfill the requirements of the fourth question are (a) the complainant chooses not to cooperate with the prosecution, (b) the offender is dead, (c) the offender is incarcerated within another jurisdiction which will not extradite.

Generally, criminal investigations can be closed in two other ways: unfounded and administratively without results.

Unfounded Complaints

> On occasion, an agency will receive a complaint that is determined through investigation to be false or baseless. If the investigation shows that no offense occurred or was attempted, the reported offense can be unfounded for UCR purposes.†

According to the UCR, these "false or baseless" reports of crimes must be verified through the investigative process. This category (unfounded) does not include cases where complainants have refused to cooperate, may have told lies about certain but not all aspects of the crime, or omitted certain information from the complaint or in cases where a successful prosecution may be in doubt. "False or baseless" means that the investigation has disclosed that no crime was committed.

1.3 Administrative Closing

Closing cases administratively with no results occurs when the investigation of the crime has failed to produce an arrest, exceptional clearance, or unfounded determination. This can happen when the identity of the offender

---

* *UCR Handbook*, p. 42.
† *UCR Handbook*, p. 40.

is unknown or the whereabouts of the offender have not been discovered. The UCR recognizes the "discontinuance of investigation and the administrative closing of cases in which all investigation has been completed"* These cases can be reopened and cleared by either arrest or by exceptional means if and when the identity or location of the offender is learned.

Whether you are conducting criminal investigations for law enforcement or defendants, it is essential to develop the variety of skills necessary for the successful completion of each case. Within this track we will cover the investigation of the UCR reported crimes as well as narcotics. We will cover crime scene response and forensic investigation, rules of evidence and chain of custody, canvassing for and the interviews of witnesses, suspect interview and interrogation techniques, working with informants, case management, "sting" operations, arrest strategies, and testimony.

* *UCR Handbook,* p. 42.

Crime Scenes

2

It may seem redundant, but crime scenes exist whenever a crime has been committed. It could be at the location of the "boiler room" telephone scam artist or at the home or office of a person sending threatening hate mail or e-mail, but more than likely the professional investigator will encounter crime scenes where a violent act or financially significant theft has occurred.

Investigations at crime scenes can generally be broken down into five areas: (1) security and safety, (2) documentation and collection of evidence, (3) detention, segregation and interview of witnesses, suspects, or persons already under arrest, (4) canvass for additional witnesses, and (5) exiting.

As a law enforcement investigator you will need to ensure that these five tasks are done in a thorough and competent manner, beginning with the freezing of the crime scene to guarantee that no further changes occur. As a criminal defense investigator you will be looking for things that should have been done, or done correctly, but weren't.

This section is written for the benefit of detective investigators with an eye on crime scenes in general and not as a primer for forensic crime scene investigators at murder scenes. Other sections of the *Professional Investigators Series* will touch on the art of forensic crime scene investigations. The concepts and methods discussed in this section of the book will be useful at any type of crime scene, be it murder, armed robbery, burglary, leaving the scene of an accident, or terrorist acts.

Manpower will be a determining factor in the procedures and sometimes in the outcome of a crime scene investigation. If you work for a medium-to-large police department and are assigned as the lead investigator of an apparent homicide, you can expect to have at least a sergeant and several other detectives, along with a crime scene unit, to assist you. If the crime is high profile, you may well have an entire task force commanded by a lieutenant or higher-ranking officer working on the case. On the other hand, if you are an investigator in a small police department, you will probably have to proceed with little or no assistance. Either way, if you are the lead investigator it will be your responsibility to ensure that the investigation proceeds correctly.

As a police investigator you should always believe that every crime you investigate will result in an arrest and that every arrest will result in a criminal trial. This will help you focus on the tasks at hand and provide you with certain guidelines to ensure that you appear professional and methodical. Keep in mind that all of the notes, reports, photographs, tape recordings, and the like that you generate during the investigation may be subject to scrutiny at trial. Therefore, before leaving for any serious crime scene, make sure you have you fresh, unused note pads, film, audiotapes, videotapes, or any other media you might be using. The worst thing you can do is contaminate your investigation with evidence from a prior investigation. Start fresh from scratch every time!

2.1 Arrival at the Scene

Upon arrival at the crime scene, take down, or request another officer or investigator to take down, the license plate numbers of vehicles parked in the area. This may aid you in identifying potential witnesses or perpetrators. Also use your powers of observation to note any onlookers who appear nervous or extraordinarily interested in the events that are occurring. Taking a moment to identify such individuals may prove worthwhile in the ensuing investigation. Take note of the time of your arrival, the weather, and anything unusual (odors, smoke, noise, and the like). Good note taking is essential throughout your time at the crime scene, so make sure to write down what you see, hear, and smell, noting time and place.

Regarding powers of observation: Yogi Berra is quoted as saying "You can observe a lot just by watching." There is a lot of truth to this statement. The powers of observation displayed by the fictional detective Sherlock Holmes appeared to be supernatural until Sir Arthur Conan Doyle took the time to explain them. Take, for example, the following exchange between Sherlock and his even more observant brother, Mycroft, as reported by Dr. Watson in *The Memoirs of Sherlock Holmes, Adventure IX—The Greek Interpreter* (http://www.bakerstreet2216.de/canon/gree.htm, originally published *Strand Magazine*, September, 1893):

> "To anyone who wishes to study mankind this is the spot," said Mycroft. "Look at the magnificent types! Look at these two men who are coming towards us, for example." "The billiard-marker and the other?" "Precisely. What do you make of the other?"

The two men had stopped opposite the window. Some chalk marks over the waistcoat pocket were the only signs of billiards which I could see in one of them. The other was a very small, dark fellow, with his hat pushed back and several packages under his arm. "An old soldier, I perceive," said Sherlock.

"And very recently discharged," remarked the brother. "Served in India, I see." "And a noncommissioned officer." "Royal Artillery, I fancy," said Sherlock. "And a widower." "But with a child." "Children, my dear boy, children." "Come," said I, laughing, "this is a little too much."

"Surely," answered Holmes, "it is not hard to say that a man with that bearing, expression of authority, and sunbaked skin, is a soldier, is more than a private, and is not long from India."

"That he has not left the service long is shown by his still wearing his ammunition boots, as they are called," observed Mycroft.

"He had not the cavalry stride, yet he wore his hat on one side, as is shown by the lighter skin on that side of his brow. His weight is against his being a sapper. He is in the artillery."

"Then, of course, his complete mourning shows that he has lost someone very dear. The fact that he is doing his own shopping looks as though it were his wife. He has been buying things for children, you perceive. There is a rattle, which shows that one of them is very young. The wife probably died in childbed. The fact that he has a picture-book under his arm shows that there is another child to be thought of."

What Yogi Berra and Sir Arthur Conan Doyle had in common was the understanding that it is possible to learn, if we pay attention. But good observation takes practice. Many of the things we see we often take for granted. You've probably heard the expression "*Too close to the forest to see the trees.*" Aside from keeping your eyes open for things that appear out of the ordinary at crime scenes, you should also pay attention to the details of the ordinary.

Perhaps you're at the death scene of an apparent suicide of a 25-year-old male who lived alone. His body is seated in a chair and slumped over the kitchen table, a bullet wound to the left temple, with obvious powder burns surrounding the entrance wound, a .38-caliber revolver in his left hand and the index finger still on the trigger. You observe a baseball bat in the corner of the room, heel up, with a glove and hat threaded over the heel and wedged down on the shaft to make carrying easier. A Yellow Pages directory lies open on the kitchen counter, next to the phone. A handwritten block-printed suicide note is on the floor, next to the kitchen table. A body, a gun, and a note — surely enough evidence to classify this as a suicide, right? But why not take a moment to look more closely? Is the baseball glove for a left-hander? If not, your antenna should now be in the fully extended position. Most people will use their dominant hand to fire a gun! Not that it is impossible to use the less dominant hand, just unlikely. Check the Yellow Pages to see what the person had been looking for. Perhaps it was opened to a suicide hotline. But what if it were opened to a TV Repair page or Sporting Goods or Chinese take-out listings? While you may not know when the page was opened, it will not be difficult to determine the last numbers called from that phone. Someone contemplating suicide may look for a suicide hotline but probably not for TV repair. These are just two examples of ordinary items that may produce extraordinary results.

Many books written by memory experts provide practice exercises to aid you in the development of observation skills. Any training in this area will pay off in both your professional life and your private life.

2.2 Documenting and Securing the Scene

Back at the crime scene, it is not possible to undo the changes that occurred prior to your arrival, but you should make every effort to identify and document what they were and who made them.

Chances are that you were not the first person to arrive at the scene, and hopefully the first responding officers were well schooled enough to secure the crime scene and prevent others, including other law enforcement per-sonnel, from entering. You should determine who was there before you, what they were doing, where they were doing it, and what if anything they touched. Identify the police officers and any other emergency service workers, relatives, friends, neighbors, or landlord. It will be very important to develop a timeline that will precede the crime by minutes, hours, or even days.

If the first officer secured evidence on his or her own or was given evidence by a third party, you should instruct the officer to safeguard it until the arrival of the forensic investigators, at which time he or she can turn it over to them so as to limit the number of persons involved in the chain of custody. You should have the officer put an identifying mark on the evidence if it will not destroy latent prints or affect laboratory tests and/or have him or her write the information on a note pad or evidence transmittal form indicating who gave it to him or her or how he or she came to be in possession of it, including time and place, and place it in a protective container with the evidence itself. If you will be conducting the search for evidence without the assistance of forensic investigators, you should take possession of the evidence, again documenting the chain of custody.

One essential tool that every investigator should bring to the crime scene is a camera. The pros and cons of digital vs. film vs. Polaroid are discussed later in this book; but for the purpose of documenting a changeable crime scene, any photograph is better than no photograph. This is especially true at changeable or unstable crime scenes, but it is a necessary step in documenting the scene as it appeared when you arrived. You must ensure that you or another investigator, police officer, or capable person take photographs of the entire scene, keeping in mind that every possible angle should be considered. It is always best to take more photos than you imagine are necessary. Photographs of the same article or location from different angles and vantage points may show you things that were not visible from other positions. Photographs should be taken of all physical evidence you can identify, making sure that the evidence is *not* moved to enhance its display. Photos should be taken of the floors, walls, ceiling, windows, doors, locks, closets, dressers, etc. These photos will greatly aid the investigator during the investigation as he or she interviews witnesses and suspects, in finding missing property, and at a subsequent trial. These photographs will not take the place of the forensic investigators' photographs.

You may also wish to videotape or use digital video to document the crime scene. The relatively small size of today's digital recorders makes them less burdensome than the shoulder-held VHS and Beta recorders of the past. I recommend disabling the sound-recording capability of these records so as to avoid any unnecessary comments from others at the scene. On the other hand, if you are confident that you can keep others from talking while you are videotaping, you may wish to make comments about the scene as you go along, thereby documenting date, time, place, evidence type and location, etc.

In addition to security at the scene, you should make a safety assessment for your own protection and the protection of anyone else that will be allowed access to the area. For example, if you are at the scene of an explosion or serious fire, you should not let anyone enter until someone with the proper expertise confirms the structural integrity. Are there any volatile or hazardous chemicals in the area? Explosives? Loaded weapons? Dangerous animals?

Crime scenes can be very confusing and emotional places, but as the investigator in charge you must bring order to the chaos. Unnecessary persons must immediately be removed and/or prevented from entering the scene, taking care not to further disturb the area. Naturally, if injured parties are present, you must allow for their medical treatment and prompt removal, but you must limit the number of persons allowed into the secure area and where they are allowed to walk.

You should secure a substantially larger area surrounding the actual crime scene and try to have only one means of entry so that unnecessary persons can be denied access and authorized persons will be forced to use one path. This is easy if your crime scene is in an apartment house but more difficult if it is in a public place. Wherever there are no natural barriers to keep people away, you will have to cordon off the enlarged crime scene area with tape, barricades, Police Crime Scene signs, or whatever is available. You will need to station at least one officer at the access point(s) to provide security and to maintain a chronological log that identifies the persons who have had or will be allowed access to the area.

Depending on the type of crime scene, you may wish to establish a command center at some point near but not connected to the crime scene. This will usually be necessary when dealing with a high-profile crime that attracts the attention of high-ranking police, fire, elected officials, and news media. Again, it is imperative to allow access to the crime scene to those who have a real need to be there. While the police commissioner may feel obligated to make his presence known, unless he is qualified as a forensic investigator and is willing to process the scene, do not let him in. These VIPs should be directed to the command post, where they can be briefed, confer with each other, or make statements to the media. It may be very difficult to keep these high-ranking police or public officials from making statements to the media, but either the investigating officer in charge or the investigative supervisor should stress the importance of releasing only the most basic information at this time. Specific information regarding MO issues, types of weapons, evidence found at the scene, etc., should not be disclosed at this point in the investigation. On the other hand, the media could be useful if the identity of the perpetrator(s) is known or if there is a physical description of the individual or the escape vehicle.

Again, these announcements and gatherings should be at a distance and out of view of the actual crime scene.

Make sure that whoever is stationed as the securing officer, or officers if there are more than one access point to the crime scene, completely understand that the only persons who should have access to the crime scene are the investigator in charge, forensic technicians, fire investigator, medical examiner, and ambulance personnel administering aid to a victim, and any specialist that has been requested by the investigating detective. Everyone else should be directed to the command post, if one has been established, or kept behind the police barricade.

One thing that most indoor crime scenes involving a residence or business have in common is that they usually contain one or more telephones, including cellular phones. It is imperative that these telephones not be touched until the arrival of the forensic technicians. They should be treated as evidence and not used to call anyone, unless it is a matter of life and death. They can hold information relating to incoming and outgoing calls as well as latent print or bodily fluid evidence. If a phone exists at an outdoor crime scene, the same caution should be exercised.

2.3 Securing and Segregating Witnesses and Suspects

As time goes by, the memories of those involved fade. Once people leave the area, they can become hard to find at a later date, so you must make every effort to identify every person associated with the scene, and if they are still at the scene you should arrange to keep them segregated and relatively uninformed about what has happened or what is currently happening. These persons will have to be observed for signs of physical evidence, such as blood splatter stains, or unique physical trace evidence that most likely could only have been transferred to them at the crime scene. They will also have to be interviewed to memorialize their stories. These statements can become useful tools during future interviews and court proceedings.

You may also need to identify and contact the person who has control of and authority over the area or, in the event of a homicide or serious injury, the next of kin.

2.4 Processing the Scene for Evidence

If the crime scene is the result of a homicide, serious assault where the victim is likely to die, armed robbery, substantial burglary/larceny, or any other situation that the investigating agency or department deems necessary, the crime scene or police lab should be requested to process the area for evidence. This may or may not have been done prior to your arrival; but if their arrival is delayed, it should not prevent you from continuing with your investigation.

Unlike characters in the now-popular TV show *C.S.I.*, forensic crime scene investigators do not interview witnesses or interrogate suspects, nor do they physically track down and apprehend criminals. Their function is locating, identifying, documenting, and collecting physical evidence, some of which will be analyzed at a laboratory. As Dr. Henry Lee and Dr. Howard A. Harris indicate in their book *Physical Evidence in Forensic Science*, "Physical evidence may be found in many places, including emergency rooms, doctors' offices, a victim's body, morgues, as records in computers or file cabinets, PDA's, cellular phones, and a myriad of other locations."[*]

It is also quite possible that multiple crime scenes exist. Just because a dead body is found in an alley, doesn't mean that the crime was committed there. Or perhaps a hit-and-run vehicle is located miles from the original accident. There can be many types of secondary crime scenes, some located nearby and others at great distances. You are the one who will be searching through records in file cabinets, personal records such as telephone books and e-mail messages, or what may turn out to be secondary crime scenes, such as businesses and residences. It will also be your responsibility, not that of the forensic investigators, to apply for search warrants where the need and probable cause exists.

2.5 Search Warrants at Crime Scenes

This section relates to warrant and warrantless searches at crime scenes only and does not address the issues of searching in connection with a lawful arrest, car stops, or plain-view seizures of contraband leading to arrest. These areas will be covered elsewhere in this manual.

Evidence that is seized illegally will be of no value. When will you not be required to obtain a search warrant? Generally, (1) when your crime scene is in a public place, (2) when permission is granted by a person with the authority to do so, (3) at a homicide scene where the victim was the only resident, (4) at scenes where emergency conditions exist, and (5) at other locations that fit certain predefined exemptions. The Fourth Amendment to the U.S. Constitution is the cornerstone that protects our citizens against "unreasonable searches and seizures." But although this is the law of the land, you must remember that state and local laws can impose stricter requirements.

Obtaining permission to conduct a search is best done in writing so that no dispute about it can arise at a later date. Keep in mind that this permission can be withdrawn with the utterance of one word: STOP!. Also, you must be certain that the person granting permission has actual authority over your crime scene. For example, let's say that you are at a death scene located in the illegal basement apartment of a one-family house. The person that has died is an illegal immigrant who resided in that apartment with his wife, who is not present at the scene. You speak with the owner of the house and tell him that you want to conduct a search not just of the area of the body, but of the entire apartment. The owner tells you that since the house is his property he will give you authorization to conduct your search, and he puts it in writing! Sounds like you can proceed with your search, right? Wrong!

' Henry Lee and Howard A. Harris, *Physical Evidence in Forensic Science* (Lawyers & Judges Publishing, 2000), p. 3.

If the deceased had lived alone you may be correct to proceed without obtaining a search warrant, but since he lived with his wife who is not present you will need to obtain her permission or apply for a search warrant.

You must always use care to determine if the person has the right to grant permission for the search of the particular area of interest. If two roommates share a two-bedroom apartment and do not share a common bedroom, neither can give permission to search the other's private living quarters.

Another important part about the giving of consent is that it must be done freely. Unlike the questioning of a suspect by the police, there is no equivalent of the Miranda decision with respect to obtaining permission to search. You will not need to inform the permission giver(s) of his/her constitutional rights, yet you cannot use trickery or deceit or coercion to obtain the permission.

The U.S. Supreme Court has ruled that the residents of a dwelling or temporary dwelling have an expectation of privacy, and while landlords may enter for certain emergencies, such as fixing leaks, in the absence of the tenant, landlords do not have the right to conduct searches of personal property or to give others that right. The same holds true for landlords of commercial property, hotel/motel owners or employees, or anyone else not having complete control and authority over the premises and its contents. Remember, federal laws are generally less restrictive than state laws, so it is recommended that you consult with your agency's legal bureau or with your local prosecutor's office to determine if a search warrant is required.

There are certain exceptions to the laws concerning search warrants, and they mainly deal with emergency situations. Whenever the immediate potential for loss of life exists, there is no requirement to obtain a search warrant. Nor is a warrant required if there is probable cause to believe that the perpetrator of a homicide or other violent crime may still be at the scene.

Searches for evidence or records at secondary locations such as a business or home of relatives or associates will require a search warrant unless authorization is obtained from a party in control of the location. When in doubt, apply for a search warrant.

When making an application for a search warrant you must provide the court with "probable cause," a particular description of the area to be searched, and a listing of the evidence that you expect to find there. You would do well to include a comprehensive list of the types of physical evidence that are ordinarily encountered at your particular crime scene. But this does not mean that you cannot seize evidence or contraband you discover during the lawful execution of your search warrant. In the event that you do encounter evidence of an unrelated crime, for example, child pornography, while you are executing a search warrant at the scene of an armed robbery, you will have the opportunity to amend your search warrant to include this new evidence.

Since rules regulating the collection and admissibility of evidence are different in federal and each state's laws, you must become familiar with rules as they apply to your jurisdiction. You can locate both federal and state rules of evidence at the following Web sites:

http://www.law.cornell.edu/rules/fre/overview.html
http://www.law.cornell.edu/statutes.html#state

According to Dr. Lee and Dr. Harris, it is imperative that certain types of evidence described as "transient" be collected immediately, without waiting for the forensic technicians. They classify "transient evidence" as "any type of physical evidence which is temporary in nature and which can easily be changed or lost."* Lee and Harris list the most common types of transient evidence as odor, temperature, imprints and identifications, and markings. Regarding the actual collection of transient physical evidence, Lee and Harris make the following recommendation:

> Transient evidence must generally be detected by the first responding officer or the first witness at the crime scene. It should be collected, recorded, and documented as soon as possible. While preservation is often not possible, most transient evidence can be recorded by notes that are verified by other observers at the scene. Certain transient evidence can be recorded by photography or videotaping; other types can be collected and preserved with special care to prevent further change or loss.†

In addition to evidence that is directly associated with the crime, you may want to secure personal telephone books of victims, computers, PDAs, cell phones, written notes, diaries, personal financial records, business records, telephone bills, answering machine tapes, digital cameras, photographs, etc., for they may provide additional leads in investigation after you leave the crime scene. Some of these items you will be able to review and analyze yourself, for example, the telephone books, diaries, and notes. Other evidence may require the use of an expert such as a forensic accountant to review business records or a computer forensic expert who can make an exact duplicate of a hard drive or other storage devices (PDAs etc.) without altering the existing information and who can then document what information there

* Henry Lee and Howard A. Harris, p. 5.
† Henry Lee and Howard A. Harris, p. 5.

is and even recover files that may have been simply deleted by hitting the Delete button yet still reside on the hard drive.

Remember, document and safeguard every piece of evidence found at the scene, recording and keeping the "chain of evidence" to the fewest persons possible.

2.6 Changeable Crime Scenes

Now that the crime scene is safe and secure and the search for physical evidence is under way, the investigator can leisurely go about business in an orderly fashion, right? Not always. Remember, crime scenes exist in every conceivable type of location, including public places, such as roadways and sidewalks, parks, trains, tunnels and bridges, stores, offices, libraries, and innumerable other locations. If your crime scene is in such a public place, your investigation will be subject to outside pressure for prompt completion so as to open the area again to normal traffic or business. Additionally, outdoor crime scenes are subject to changing weather conditions. If it appears that the crime scene will be altered or destroyed by weather or other external factors before the forensic technicians arrive, the investigator should take the necessary steps to collect and document any specific physical evidence and the entire crime scene in general.

It is certainly best to have the forensic technicians document the scene with photographs and sketches and to collect the evidence, but it is not always practical. There may also be occasions when forensic investigators are not available. Ultimately, it is the responsibility of the lead investigator to ensure that physical evidence is located, documented, and collected from the crime scene and from sources outside of the primary crime scene as well.

In order to do an effective search for evidence, you will need a plan and perhaps some additional equipment. Good lighting is essential for your search, so in the absence of light you will need to bring in a portable light source, making sure to do no damage to the scene. Since you cannot control where crime scenes exist, you may need to bring a portable generator to scenes where electricity is unavailable, for example, remote outdoor scenes and abandoned properties.

Once you have sufficient light, you will want to decide on the best search pattern to utilize at your scene. You may decide on a grid search, where you systematically search a small area of your crime scene before moving on to the next, adjoining area. You may decide to perform a search using concentric circles that continually expand outward from the center point of your crime scene. There is no correct method to use, but having no method will lead to a disorganized and inefficient search that will leave you open to criticism, especially at a trial.

Some agencies will provide their investigators with an evidence-collection kit, while others will not. As an investigator you would do well to make sure that you have such a kit available to you, whether or not your department supplies it. In addition to a camera and plenty of color and black-and-white film, you should bring this kit with you to crime scenes, keeping it in the car until it becomes necessary to use it. At a minimum this kit should contain the following: (1) surgical gloves to protect you from AIDS and other infectious diseases and to prevent you from depositing your own fingerprints at the crime scene, (2) black, white, and magnetic latent print powders, a powder application brush, lifting tape, and backing cards, (3) 8″ × 10″ sealable manila envelopes for transportation and chain-of-custody purposes, (4) smaller paper envelopes, metal containers, as well as pharmacy folded paper sheets, (5) Ziploc® bags, (6) forceps, (7) a small scraping tool, (8) fingerprint cards and portable inkpad, (9) a clean eyedropper. You may also want to keep a supply of Handy Wipes to clean up afterwards.

In changeable crime scenes you may be required to collect many types of physical evidence prior to the arrival of the forensic technicians. It is important to have a basic knowledge of collection techniques and the proper way to store the evidence. Remember, you probably do not have the training of a forensic technician; but if the alternative is to handle the collection of physical evidence or face its destruction, you should use whatever means is available to prudently collect and preserve the evidence. Each piece of evidence should be placed in its own container, individually marked, numbered, and labeled with the case number, date, time, and location where it was discovered, and sealed in an envelope or protective container that can be initialed or signed by the person who collected it.

If you have no other choice but to collect blood or other type of bodily fluid evidence prior to the arrival of the forensic technicians, you should first photograph the evidence extensively, from all conceivable angles. Extra care should be taken to photographically document any patterns made by blood, for use in later reconstruction. Once you have completed the photography, you should begin collection.

If there is liquid blood at the scene, you will need to gather as much of it as possible into a clean container. Use the earlier-referenced evidence-collection kit if you have one; but if you don't, you will probably have to improvise. Again, this is a last-resort situation where the evidence will not survive without immediate collection! If your crime scene is located outside on a street, you may be able to obtain a glass, paper, or plastic container, drinking cup, empty soup container, or other vessel designed to hold a liquid. If you are unable to get a clean eyedropper, you may consider using a clean plastic spoon or other utensil to transfer the liquid blood into your vessel. Once you have collected as much blood as possible, you should cover the container with a material that will allow air to penetrate. You do not want to seal the container in such a way as to induce condensation. Make sure to keep the evidence container away from heat and to give it to the forensic technicians as soon as they arrive, carefully documenting the chain of custody. If a secure refrigerator is located at the crime scene, you should place the container inside it. If it is not possible for you to collect the liquid blood, Dr. Lee and Dr. Harris make a suggestion: "Place a clean white cotton swatch in the liquid blood, allow it to dry, and then package it in paper"[*] Naturally you may not have a clean white cotton swatch at your disposal, so improvisation will be required. Again, any sample is better than no sample at all, so I recommend utilizing any clean absorbent material at your disposal —cotton T-shirt, a cigarette filter, etc.

If you are collecting dried blood or other bodily fluid, it is best to take the entire piece of material, for example, a shirt or pants, rather than cutting out pieces. Again, this is assuming a changeable crime scene in which the evidence must be collected and safeguarded to prevent destruction. Since your evidence-collection kit has only small paper envelopes, improvisation will again be necessary if you are to safeguard large pieces of evidence. Perhaps you can obtain a shopping bag from a local store and use it for any large article such as a pair of pants. If no large containers are available, you could cut the dried bloodstained area and secure it in a smaller envelope. If the bloodstain is on something solid, like a wall or a bathtub, you should take scrapings and place them into a piece of paper and then into a paper envelope. Again, prior to scraping you must photograph, photograph, photograph!

Dr. Lee and Dr. Harris make the following recommendation with respect to the collection of blood evidence:

> Clothing: 1. Clothing that is wet with blood or any body fluid should be allowed to air dry naturally. 2. Mark identification data away from the stained areas on the garment. 3. Package all clothing in clean wrapping paper or paper bags. Always avoid folding garments through stained area. 4. Under no circumstance should technicians place this type of evidence in any plastic or airtight container, since retained moisture will speed putrefaction of the biological stain evidence, often making it useless for analysis. 5. Do not shake out the clothing as it is packaged. If articles are found in a pile, note their order in the pile as they are picked up. They should be packaged individually since this information may

[*] Henry Lee and Howard A. Harris, p. 52.

aid in the reconstruction of the crime. 6. With living victims where
it becomes necessary to cut the clothing off, avoid cutting through
the pattern area or through holes that may have been caused by
a bullet or weapon, as this will destroy valuable physical evidence.[*]

Physical Evidence in Forensic Science, on pages 50–52, provides three
excellent tables related to the collection of blood evidence at crime scenes
that are designed to aid forensic technicians, but they may be of interest to
you as well.

Once again, if your choice is between doing nothing and losing the crime
scene evidence and doing something to document, collect, and preserve it
even though you do not possess all of the technical expertise of a trained
forensic technician, then do something. The courts will usually view your
reasonable and good intentions in a positive light.

2.7 Stable Crime Scenes

If your crime scene is indoors and/or not subject to change, you should not
attempt to handle or locate any evidence; rather, you should await the arrival
of the forensic investigators. It is also possible that the forensic investigators
may have arrived at the scene before you. Either way, you should identify the
lead forensic investigator and conduct a walk through of the scene. This will
provide both of you with a basic understanding of what has happened, where
the physical evidence may be located, and the best way for you and them to
move around the scene without altering it.

If you have already secured physical evidence prior to the arrival of
forensic investigators, now is the time to turn it over. Alternatively, you may
choose to maintain custody of any evidence already in your possession and
deliver it personally to the laboratory or property clerk for safekeeping. In
either event, you must clearly document the chain of custody of every piece
of evidence you have handled. The following guidelines are from the National
Institute of Justice's *Death Investigation: A Guide for the Scene Investigator*
regarding the chain of custody for physical evidence:

6. Establish Chain of Custody

Principle: Ensuring the integrity of the evidence by establishing
and maintaining a chain of custody is vital to an investigation.
This will safeguard against subsequent allegations of tampering,
theft, planting, and contamination of evidence.

---

[*] Henry Lee and Howard A. Harris, p. 49.

Policy: Prior to the removal of any evidence, the custodian(s) of evidence shall be designated and shall generate and maintain a chain of custody for all evidence collected.

Procedure: Throughout the investigation, those responsible for preserving the chain of custody should:

A. Document location of the scene and time of arrival of the death investigator at the scene.

B. Determine custodian(s) of evidence, determine which agency(ies) is/are responsible for collection of specific types of evidence, and determine evidence collection priority for fragile/fleeting evidence.

C. Identify, secure, and preserve evidence with proper containers, labels, and preservatives.

D. Document the collection of evidence by recording its location at the scene, time of collection, and time and location of disposition.

E. Develop personnel lists, witness lists, and documentation of times of arrival and departure of personnel.

2.8 Crime Scene Summary

It is essential to maintain a proper chain of custody for evidence. Through proper documentation, collection, and preservation, the integrity of the evidence can be assured. A properly maintained chain of custody and prompt transfer will reduce the likelihood of a challenge to the integrity of the evidence."*

While the National Institute of Justice's *Death Investigation: A Guide for the Scene Investigator* speaks specifically about death investigations, the recommendations for the collection of evidence should not vary during the investigation of other major crimes.

Once you ensure that the crime scene is secure and is being processed by the forensic investigators, you can begin to move on to the remaining two

---

* Title: Death Investigation: A Guide for the Scene Investigator. Series: Research Report Author: National Medicolegal Review Panel, *Death Investigation: A Guide for the Scene Investigator* (National Institute of Justice, November 1999).

areas of your crime scene investigation: the interviewing of witnesses, suspects, or persons under arrest, and the canvass for additional witnesses.

Police investigators must always keep in mind that their actions will be scrutinized by defense counsel at trial and that any failure or deviations from generally accepted investigative principals may serve to discredit or embarrass them during testimony. The issues of proper documentation and chain of evidence cannot be stressed enough. For those of you who may think that too much emphasis is placed on these items, I suggest you review the issues surrounding the case of *The People of the State of California v. Orenthal James (O.J.) Simpson.*

2.9 Witnesses

If things have gone well, you have been able to identify and segregate any witnesses and suspects that were present at the original crime scene. In a best-case scenario they would have been transported back to your office to await interview or interrogation. But if their transportation is not possible or practical, they should be segregated in an area away from and out of view of the original crime scene until you are ready to interview them. This is not to say that you shouldn't speak to a suspect who is found at the scene distraught and shaking his head, holding a bloody knife, and wearing blood-soaked clothing. In the absence of a spontaneous confession from this type of individual, Miranda warnings are certainly in order at that moment. But more often than not you will be better served to collect as much information about the crime as possible prior to interviewing or interrogating anyone so that the information you have collected can be used to confirm or discredit their recollections.

Interview and interrogation techniques will be covered elsewhere in this book, but, as with any inquiry into the commission of a crime, you must seek the answers to the basic questions of who, what, why, where, when, and how. Your advantage at this point is that the person(s) you are about to speak with do not know how much you have learned at the scene, nor do they know who else you have spoken with or what has been told to you by others. They should have been kept away from others and should not have been aware of what you or other investigators have been doing.

In addition to interviews and memorialized statements, you should obtain a set of rolled fingerprints and palm prints from each individual who had access to the crime scene and from any suspect, for comparison purposes to latent-print lifts.

2.10 Canvassing

In a perfect world it would be best to conduct the interviews of existing witnesses, suspects, and persons under arrest prior to conducting the canvass for additional witnesses, since information obtained during the canvass may serve to substantiate or discredit their accounts. However, practical issues such as manpower availability, time of day or night, and location of the crime scene will probably dictate that the canvass be conducted sooner rather than later. With that in mind it is essential that the investigator(s) conducting the canvass have as complete a picture as possible of the crime scene and any events leading up to it, including but not limited to descriptions of possible perpetrators, modus operandi, noises or sounds (gunshots, screams, drilling, etc.), odors (smoke, accelerants, body decomposition), escape routes, geographic location, and sequence and time of events. Armed with this knowledge, the canvassing investigator may be able to identify bits of information from persons who may not know that they possess it.

The initial canvass should be conducted in a logical manner, especially in high-density-population locations such as hi-rise apartment or office buildings, and thoroughly documented so that follow-up canvasses for anyone missed during the initial efforts, and reinterviews of those persons having useful information will not be overlooked.

In addition to finding someone who may have seen, heard, or smelled something, a canvass may locate a witness who provides information on possible suspects, motives, the victim's friends or enemies, the victim's habits, or persons with access to the crime scene. The canvassing investigator must also keep in mind that the perpetrator may live or work in the immediate area, so it is conceivable that you may knock on his/her door as well. Again, the powers of observation can be of great assistance to the detective during this part of the investigation. Observe the demeanor of the people that you speak with. Are they unnecessarily nervous or overly inquisitive? Does their clothing appear to have trace evidence, or is it torn? Does the person have any sign of recent injury?

As discussed earlier, wherever practical and within the boundaries of common sense, every person who was present at the crime scene upon the arrival of the first officers should have been detained and segregated. Reality and practicality suggest that crime scenes at mass gatherings, such as sporting events and concerts, do not result in locking the doors to keep people from leaving. If your crime scene were in the midst of large numbers of people, I would recommend taking extensive photographs of the crowds nearest to your scene so that you can review them at a later date and compare them to any suspects you may develop during the investigation. With the assistance of other investigators or police officers, an immediate canvass should be made to identify as many people as possible in the immediate vicinity, for future interviews.

2.11 Exit, Release, or Continue Securing the Scene

How you leave the crime scene will depend on the type of crime and its location. For example, if you are investigating the theft of precious art from a museum, you will need to secure the premises until someone of authority arrives so as to prevent further thefts. If you are at the scene of a building explosion, you will need to seek out someone of competent authority to determine if the building is safe to return to or if it should be closed pending review by the local building department. One thing in common at most every crime scene is that someone will ask, "What happens next?"

As the investigator in charge, you must be able to explain to victims or family members what will happen next and what if anything they will need to do. At burglaries you may tell the victim(s) that you will be submitting to the crime lab any latent prints as well as the comparison prints of the victims or anyone else with legitimate access and that you will be visiting local pawn shops to locate their property. You may also suggest that the victims visit these pawn shops as well and contact you directly if they recognize their property. You may tell them that you will be reviewing and continually monitoring other crimes in the area to determine if the same MO was/is used. Remind them that they should prepare an exact list of stolen articles for you and to forward the list to their insurance company and include the loss on their federal income tax return.

At robbery scenes, sex crime scenes, or any other scene where the victims or witnesses were able to view the perpetrator(s), in addition to telling them about latent prints and MOs, you will want to have them look at photographs at your identification unit or office. You should also let them know that you may bring photo arrays to them in the future. They should be told what to do in the event that they see the perpetrator(s) again, for example, call 911, write down license plate numbers, try to avoid confrontation prior to police arrival, and observe clothing, activities (food shopping, banking, etc.), direction of travel, and associates.

Once you have completed your investigation at the scene, including any forensic crime scene processing, you should be able to turn control of the area back to the appropriate persons. You should make sure that you or the forensic investigators remove all evidence and equipment and try to leave the area in the best condition possible under the circumstances.

In the event that you feel the need to return to the crime scene at a later time for further investigation, you will need to continue security. Certainly the best way to ensure security is to station an officer at the scene. Secondarily, you may wish to post tamper-proof "crime scene — do not enter" signs on locked windows and doors, keeping in mind that this is the least secure method of keeping people from entering the scene. If, when you return, the seals have been broken, you can rest assured that any evidence you subsequently retrieve will likely be precluded as evidence at any trial. If you wish to maintain security over a crime scene for an extended period of time, that is, days or weeks, you will more than likely need to apply for a court order granting you such control. You should consult with your department's legal bureau or the local prosecutor's office for assistance in such matters. Even in cases were decedents resided alone, there will be issues such as returning possession to a landlord, wills, and probate filings.

Homicide scenes are certainly the most emotional of all crime scenes, and how you leave the scene can have a dramatic effect if family members are present. The National Institute of Justice's *Death Investigation: A Guide for the Scene Investigator* makes the following recommendation with respect to dealing with families upon your exit from a death scene:

4. Assist the Family

Principle: The investigator provides the family with a timetable so they can arrange for final disposition and provides information on available community and professional resources that may assist the family.

Authorization: Medical Examiner/Coroner Official Office Policy Manual; state or federal statutory authority.

Policy: The investigator shall offer the decedent's family information regarding available community and professional resources.

Procedure: When the investigator is assisting the family, it is important to:

A. Inform the family if an autopsy is required.

B. Inform the family of available support services (e.g., victim assistance, police, social services, etc.).

C. Inform the family of appropriate agencies to contact with questions (medical examiner/coroner offices, law enforcement, SIDS support group, etc.).

D. Ensure family is not left alone with body (if circumstances warrant).

E. Inform the family of approximate body release timetable.

F. Inform the family of information release timetable (toxicology, autopsy results, etc., as required).

G. Inform the family of available reports, including cost, if any.

Summary: The interaction with the family allows the investigator to assist and direct them to appropriate resources. It is essential that families be given a timetable of events so that they can make necessary arrangements. In addition, the investigator needs to make them aware of what and when information will be available.*

2.12 Crime Scene Checklist

1. Secure the Crime Scene
2. Allow for treatment of injured
3. Maintain, or have maintained a chronological/locational log
4. Identify those that came before you to establish time-line
5. Segregate, interview and memorialize witness statements
6. Notify Forensic Crime Scene to process area
7. Follow-up on physical evidence located in personal records or outside of the original crime scene, e.g., doctor's offices
8. Collect transient physical evidence
9. Some crime scenes are in public places and speed is necessary
10. Exterior crime scenes can be altered by weather, so use a camera to document if forensic technicians have not yet arrived
11. Have an evidence-collection kit available
12. Collect vulnerable physical evidence that can be damaged or altered by weather or other external forces
13. Improvise collection methods for blood evidence only when absolutely necessary
14. Conduct walk-through with forensic investigator
15. Chain of custody
16. Interview witnesses/suspects/arrestees

---

* National Institute of Justice, *Death Investigation: A Guide for the Scene Investigator* (November 1999).

17. Conduct precanvass briefing, and canvass
18. Exit the scene

Death Investigations

3

Why do people die? From an investigative, nonmedical standpoint, there can be only four possible reasons for death: (1) natural causes (including disease), (2) accidental (including natural disasters), (3) suicide, and (4) homicide. There are, however, many causes of death. The National Center for Health Statistics of the CDC (Centers for Disease Control) provided the following table:[*]

Number of Deaths for Leading Causes of Death (United States, 2001)

Heart disease: 700,142
Cancer: 553,768
Stroke: 163,538
Chronic lower respiratory diseases: 123,013
Accidents (unintentional injuries): 101,537
Diabetes: 71,372
Influenza/pneumonia: 62,034
Alzheimer's disease: 53,852
Nephritis, nephrotic syndrome, and nephrosis: 39,480
Septicemia: 32,238

Well, it doesn't appear that murder has made the list. However, suicide did make it to number 11 on CDC's list, with a total of 30,622 cases for 2001.

So how many homicides are there? "The U.S. Centers for Disease Control reports that in 2001, there were a total of 20,308 deaths from homicide in the United States."[†]

Since 2,416,425 deaths were recorded in the United States during calendar year 2001,[‡] it appears that less than 1% were the result of homicides, and

[*] National Center for Health Statistics, *Deaths: Final Data for 2001*, Vol. 50, No. 3 (Hyattsville, MD: Author, Sept. 18, 2003), Table C, p. 8.
[†] National Center for Health Statistics, Table C, p. 8.
[‡] National Center for Health Statistics, Table C, p. 8.

that includes the horrific events of 9/11. Unfortunately, there are no statistics that reveal where all of these 2 million deaths occurred. Surely many occurred in health care facilities and were never reported to the police, but a great number of deaths occurred outside of hospitals — on the streets, in homes, at businesses, and in public places.

3.1 Death by Natural Causes

The cause of death in the vast majority of cases will be determined by the deceased's private physician or the hospital/health care physician who has treated the person as a patient and who will sign the death certificate. In cases that involve suspicious, unknown-reason, or accidental deaths, the case will usually be referred to the medical examiner (M.E.) or coroner for autopsy. In addition to the cause of death, the M.E., or coroner will also reach a conclusion regarding the mode of or reason for the death. As the investigator, you will have no official input into the determination of cause, but your investigation can have a profound impact on the determination of the mode or method. It is one thing for an infant to stop breathing (sudden infant death syndrome, SIDS) and quite another if a pillow was held over the infant's mouth and nose.

Of the cases that are referred to the coroner or M.E., as long as the autopsy can conclude that death was not caused by some outside influence such as trauma, drugs, or weapons, but rather by some sudden physiological change or a disease, then the cause will be noted as natural and the police investigator will have little if anything to do with this matter.

When a person calls 911 to report a death or near death of an individual, a police officer is usually dispatched along with the ambulance. What happens next will effect the direction and possibly the result of any investigation that may follow. This book is written for the benefit of the professional investigators, be they police, private detectives, insurance investigators, or the like. Since it is within the domain of the police to investigate all deaths in public places and all suspicious deaths regardless of location, private and insurance investigators would do well to become acquainted with police investigative procedures in general, and specifically their local police department's policies with respect to death investigations. This will ensure a system of checks and balances that can aid in the proper investigation of death cases.

3.2 Accidental Deaths

Aside from physical illness and disease, accidents account for more deaths than any other cause. As we know from the CDC's statistics for 2001, deaths due to accidental injuries numbered 101,537. By far, the leading cause of accidental deaths occurred during transportation-related accidents (47,288). Police departments will conduct investigations of all fatal motor vehicle accidents to ensure that no criminality was involved. These types of accident investigations or reconstructions are conducted by police officers or investigators who have usually received specialized training. The results of their investigations are usually provided to the local prosecutor or district attorney, who will ultimately decide whether or not to prosecute. Police and other agencies, such as the National Transportation Safety Board (NTSB) and the Federal Aviation Administration (FAA) will investigate accidents involving trains and airplanes. Overwhelmingly, these types of investigations result in civil rather than criminal prosecutions.

Other types of accidental deaths can be caused by falls, becoming caught between or struck by objects and machinery, drowning, accidental firearms discharge, animal bites, insect bites, electrocutions, fires, and dozens of additional causes. While some of these deaths will obviously be accidental, good police procedures should not be ignored.

As the police investigator, you will usually not be the first officer at a death scene. As already stated, a uniformed officer will generally be dispatched to a death scene under several possible scenarios: (1) a 911 caller indicates there has been a homicide, (2) an accident, (3) a suicide, (4) unknown cause of death. The officer responding to this dispatch should understand that his or her responsibilities at homicide scenes include the protection of life, the apprehension of perpetrators, the detention of suspects and witnesses, and the preservation of the crime scene, usually in that order. But we now know that homicides make up less that 1% of all deaths, so how often will the responding officer practice these responsibilities? Hopefully every time he or she responds to a death scene. By treating every death as suspicious, there will less room for error.

At the New York Police Department, a complaint report was prepared for every reported death of an individual of which the department was made aware. This included deaths in public places, residences, businesses, etc. This complaint report was classified as an "Investigation of a DOA [dead on arrival]" and was referred to the corresponding police precinct's detective unit for investigation. Most every police department will have a similar procedure to ensure that deaths that are not witnessed or attested to by doctors as having occurred by natural causes are investigated.

In many cases, these "investigate DOA" assignments are treated as a formality. For example, an individual walking down the street who grabs his/her chest while falling to the ground will usually be transported to the hospital as soon as the ambulance arrives. The first officer on the scene may have arrived before the ambulance, in which case he/she may have provided cardiopulmonary resuscitation (CPR), or the officer may have arrived after the ambulance has left for the hospital with the patient. Either way, the police officer should end up at the hospital and obtain the pertinent information regarding the identity of the victim, the treating physician, time of death, and notification of next of kin. The detective may not learn about this type of death for many hours or perhaps even the next day. The detective investigation should include the review of the complaint report, the interview of the reporting officer, identification of the victim if not already done by the reporting officer, and notification to next of kin if not already done. If nothing suspicious appears during this initial investigation, the investigator will more than likely wait for the autopsy results from the medical examiner or coroner before continuing or closing the investigation.

During these "routine" cases, the first officer will generally not be concerned with safeguarding the scene. He should have taken the names of any witnesses or of the 911 caller if that person is still present. But other than the personal belongings of the victim, the officer will generally not remove or protect anything at the scene. If at a later date the medical examiner provides information that classifies the death as suspicious or a homicide, for example, an unseen wound, or toxicology report that indicates poisoning, then the detective will begin the investigation without the benefit of a secure primary crime scene.

On the other hand, every suspicious or suicide death scene should be treated as a homicide scene until it is determined to be otherwise. These scenes are as varied as one can imagine. For example, the death scene may be at a train station, where the body is located on the tracks beneath a train that was pulling into or out of the station.

3.3 Suicides

An investigator will generally encounter four types of death scenes, and he/she must be able to reach an informed conclusion within a reasonable amount of time. Was this death natural? accidental? suicidal? homicidal? As a general rule, at apparent suicides the scene must be secured, the safety of all persons who are present must be a primary consideration, evidence must be safeguarded, witnesses must be identified and detained, and suspects must be detained or arrested where probable cause exists. While these things are within the domain of the first officers and their supervisors, the detective must be aware of them and ensure that they have been done. In addition to forensic or crime scene investigators, there may be a need for other specialized units trained in emergency rescue procedures or railroad personnel who can ensure that the power has been turned off. Unless there are credible witnesses who will verify that the victim jumped to death rather than being pushed, this should be treated as a homicide crime scene.

Other suicide death scenes can include gunshots, hangings, drowning, jumping from high places, carbon monoxide in vehicles or homes, knife/razor wounds, poisoning, explosive devices/fireworks, and death by police (yes, it is not uncommon for individuals to force police officers to kill them).

As in any other situation, the protection of life should be the primary concern and is the only permissible reason to alter the scene when confronted by an apparent suicide. If the victim is displaying any signs of life, the officer must take appropriate action, be it removing the victim from a bathtub filled with water to administer CPR or stopping the bleeding at a wrist slashing. If this means altering evidence, so be it. But the officer can minimize the destruction or alteration of evidence in many ways. For example, if a hanging victim must be cut down, the location of the cut should be away from the knot if possible; subsequently the material should be collected as evidence, with documentation by the officer of when, how, and exactly where he cut it.

In his book *Practical Homicide Investigation: Tactics, Procedures, and Forensic Techniques,* Vernon J. Geberth discusses the first officer's obligation to "the protection of life": "However, under ordinary circumstances, wherever there is any doubt as to death, the officer should presume that there is life and proceed accordingly. First officers should, therefore, be aware of the signs of death"[*] Geberth goes on to list and describe the following physiological indicators that police officers can observe to determine if a person is alive or dead: "Breath stoppage, cessation of pulse, and eye reflexes" as well as the obvious signs of death, such as "rigor mortis, lividity, and putrefaction"[†]

There are many sources of information relating to the changes that occur in the human body after death, but for an authoritative reference, you need to go no further than Chapter 9 of *Practical Homicide Investigation: Tactics, Procedures, and Forensic Techniques.*

As the investigator, you should be aware of all changes that have occurred at the suicide scene and who caused them. Upon your arrival at a possible suicide scene you should thoroughly interview the first officer(s), to determine what the scene appeared like on their arrival, what was told to them by persons who were present, what actions they took, and the changes that have occurred. If any "suicide notes" were left, they should be treated as physical evidence and secured without excessive handling. You should determine the identities of all the persons who handled the note, in the event that

[*] Vernon J. Geberth, *Practical Homicide Investigations: Tactics, Procedures, and Forensic Techniques,* 2nd ed. (Elsevier Science, 1990.), p. 31.
[†] Vernon J. Geberth, pp. 32, 33.

it becomes necessary to obtain comparison prints for any latent prints that may be found on it. This note should also be considered a questioned document that may require future handwriting analysis.

As with any other crime scene, you should take extensive notes of your observations, including what you smell. Take photographs of the body in general and of the area surrounding any wounds or marks in particular, of the general area of the potential crime scene, doors, locks, windows, and furniture, much as you would at a homicide scene. Bodies will decompose at varying rates, depending on climatic conditions. Odors that accompany the decay of a human body can be overpowering and are sometimes the reason for the discovery of the body itself. Many calls to 911 for "smell of gas" or other noxious odors are the result of decomposing bodies. Invariably at scenes where decomposing bodies are found, the first thought will be to open the windows. As at any crime scene, the condition of the windows, doors, and locks must be observed, documented, and processed for evidence.

If family or friends are present, you must keep them away from the potential crime scene area. You must find out what they have touched and if they moved the body or altered the scene in any way. Many times family members or friends will alter suicide scenes to protect the honor of the victim or the family, to preserve life insurance payouts, or to cover up a homicide. If they are trying to cover up a suicide, they may remove or clean weapons, remove or destroy suicide notes, or make the scene appear to be a break-in homicide. If they are trying to cover up a homicide, they may just add weapons and notes and try to cover up signs of a struggle or break-in. You must keep these issues in mind when you interview them.

For the most part the families of suicide victims will be grieving and highly emotional. There is no easy way to interview them, but it is necessary and unavoidable. As an investigator, you must be compassionate yet skeptical enough to keep an eye open for inconsistencies or facts that would indicate homicide rather than suicide.

When interviewing the family or friends of an apparent suicide victim you should try to determine who was the last person to be with the victim and the victim's physical and mental condition. Working backwards, you will want to establish a timeline for the victim to determine where and with who he/she has been.

It is widely accepted in the mental health field that depression is the leading cause of suicide. Keeping this in mind, you will also want to develop a more historical medical and emotional background for the victim and determine if there have been any recent life-altering events. This can be aided by an inspection of the medicines in the residence and calendars with doctor or attorney appointments, but usually relatives and friends will supply this type of background. You should pay attention to information about a serious mental or physical illness, the death of spouse, a recent or impending divorce, business or legal troubles, the loss of a job, recent retirement, the recent death of a friend, changes in behaviors and habits such as eating or sleeping, previous suicide attempts, bouts of depression, talk of suicide, giving away possessions, etc. In school-age victims, you may become aware of the stress associated with studying for exams, sexual identity issues, rejection issues, and other psychological problems that are common with adolescents. But beware, you may also learn that the person had enemies or that recent threats had made against him/her.

The NIJ's *Death Investigation: A Guide for the Scene Investigator* proposes the following procedure as part of the death investigation:

4. Document Decedent Mental Health History

Principle: The decedent's mental health history can provide insight into the behavior/state of mind of the individual. That insight may produce clues that will aid in establishing the cause, manner, and circumstances of the death.

Authorization: medical examiner/coroner official office policy manual; state or federal statutory authority.

Policy: The investigator shall obtain information from sources familiar with the decedent pertaining to the decedent's mental health history.

Procedure: The investigator should:

A. Document the decedent's mental health history, including hospitalizations and medications.

B. Document the history of suicidal ideations, gestures, and/or attempts.

C. Document mental health professionals (e.g., psychiatrists, psychologists, counselors, etc.) who treated the decedent.

D. Document family mental health history.

Summary: Knowledge of the mental health history allows the investigator to evaluate properly the decedent's state of mind and

contributes to the determination of cause, manner, and circumstances of death[*].

3.4 Causes for Suspicion

As the investigator, you should remain at the scene until the medical examiner
or coroner arrives and then give him or her a complete briefing of your
investigation. You should accompany the medical examiner as he/she con-
ducts an examination of the body, taking careful note of the findings. His/her
examination should provide you with an approximate time of death, a preliminary cause of death pending autopsy, and if in his opinion the death
appears suspicious. With experience, an investigator will be able to learn to
estimate the time of death based on certain physical changes to the body after
death. For example, rigor mortis is generally described as the stiffening of
the body after death. Under normal climate and physical circumstances, this
"stiffening" will not begin to exhibit itself until approximately 3 hours after
death and will generally fade away after 36 hours.

Body temperature can be another indication of estimated time of death,
because the exterior skin temperature will reach the temperature of the
surrounding area within 8–12 hours after death. The body's internal temperature will lose heat more slowly, but the general rule under normal conditions
is the loss of 1.5° per hour. This is not to say that you should insert a
thermometer into the body. Rather, the medical examiner will generally use
an anal thermometer to register the internal temperature, and in conjunction
with the state of rigor mortis and other factors, he may be able to provide
the estimated time of death. An approximate time of death that does not
conform to the timeline you have constructed based on interviews of witnesses, family, friends, telephone calls/logs, or other documentation is reason
for suspicion.

Other changes to the body, or lack of changes, will be of interest at some
suicide scenes as well. For example, carbon monoxide (CO) poisoning results
in a cherry-red skin coloration, or "lividity." The lack of this phenomenon
in cases where CO poisoning appears to be the mode of death should give
rise to suspicion of another cause of death. Carbon monoxide needs to be
inhaled in order for this cherry-red lividity to occur. It cannot occur postmortem.

Postmortem lividity, or livor mortis, is caused by the effect of gravity on
the blood and begins immediately after circulation stops. Blood will begin
to settle in the lowest parts of the body as it responds to the earth's gravi-

[*] National Institute of Justice, *Death Investigation: A Guide for the Scene Investigator*
(November 1999).

tational pull and will be noticeable by the dark purplish color of the skin. Therefore, a body found hanging from the feet will show this lividity in the head and upper body. Interestingly, blood will not leave this after-death trademark on any parts of the body that are in direct contact with a solid surface; rather, you can expect to see pale patches in these areas. Postmortem lividity will generally leave a permanent stain on the body after 10–12 hours. Finding this type of discoloration on any part of the body, suggesting that it has defied gravity, is certainly grounds for suspicion that the body has been moved.

The presence or lack of *petechial hemorrhages* (small pin-sized red dots that occur as the result of smothering or asphyxiation) on the face, near the eyes, or inside the eyelids of an alleged suicide-by-hanging victim could serve as confirmation of or reason for suspicion. You would expect to find these hemorrhages on a hanging victim but not on one who appears to have died from a drug overdose or gunshot wounds.

Another change that begins to occur in the human body immediately after death is decomposition, also known as *putrefaction:*

> Putrefaction is the postmortem destruction of the soft tissues of the body by the action of bacteria and enzymes (both bacterial and endogenous). Tissue breakdown resulting from the action of endogenous enzymes alone is known as autolysis. Putrefaction results in the gradual dissolution of the tissues into gases, liquids, and salts. The main changes that can be recognized in the tissues undergoing putrefaction are changes in color, the evolution of gases, and liquefaction.*

It is this "evolution of gases" that creates the odor of death in bodies with advanced decomposition. At normal temperatures, this odor may take up to a week to develop, but with the higher temperatures and humidity found in un-air-conditioned areas during a hot summer, it may occur much more rapidly. For an in-depth description of postmortem changes, I recommend that you visit the University of Dundee's website at http://www.dundee.ac.uk/forensicmedicine/llb/timedeath.htm.

Wounds on the body can also give rise to suspicion in apparent suicide investigations. In general, the types of wounds you will observe at death investigations will have been caused by guns, knifes or other penetrating or cutting-type weapons, including glass, ropes, and other ligature materials, and striking-type instruments, such as bats, hammers, and rocks. The following table, from the CDC's *National Vital Statistics Reports,* shows that

---

* University of Dundee, *Postmortem Changes and Time of Death,* http://www.dundee.ac.uk/forensicmedicine/llb/timedeath.htm

the number of suicide deaths by gunshot accounts for nearly half of all suicides.[*]

Mortality from Suicides (United States, 2001)

All Suicides
Number of deaths: 30,622
Deaths per 100,000 population: 10.8
Firearm suicides
Number of deaths: 16,869
Deaths per 100,000 population: 5.9
Suffocation suicides
Number of deaths: 6,198
Deaths per 100,000 population: 2.2
Poisoning suicides
Number of deaths: 5,191
Deaths per 100,000 population: 1.8

3.5 Gunshot Wounds

From the preceding statistics, it is apparent that the weapon of choice for suicide victims is the firearm, which causes more than 50% of all suicide deaths.

When viewing gunshot wounds on alleged suicide victims you should expect to see contact or near-contact wounds to the head or torso. Contact or near-contact wounds to any other part of the body should be cause for suspicion.

Contact wounds will not have scattered gunshot residue surrounding the wound since the unburned powder will generally follow the projectile into the wound. Because of the flame and smoke produced from the barrel of the firearm and the friction of the projectile passing through the skin, you can expect to find burn marks and irregular edges at the entrance to the wound and a grimy or sooty deposit around it. Contact wounds to bony parts of the body, such as the skull, will be larger and ragged, often resembling the shape of a star. Both contact and near-contact wounds may be encircled by a discoloration, or "abrasion collar," that is caused by damage to the tissue as the projectile passes through the skin. Muzzle imprints on the skin are also common in contact wounds, sometimes providing a very clear picture of the barrel of the weapon that was used.

Close-range but noncontact gunshot wounds generally appear to be round and usually are smaller than the actual size of the bullet. The reason that the entrance wound may appear smaller than the actual bullet is that the skin is

Deaths: Final Data for 200,1 Table 18, Vol. 52, No. 3.

elastic and if the bullet enters the body in a fleshy area, the skin will stretch as it is being penetrated, closing back up behind it. These noncontact but close-range gunshot wounds will show gunpowder and other discharge items embedded into the skin and/or cause hemorrhaging around the wound. This residue is pushed into the skin by the force of the energy emitted from the barrel, as is the hemorrhaging caused by the impact of foreign particles in the residue stream. As the distance between the wound and the barrel increases, this energy dissipates. Any alleged gunshot-suicide wound that does not show signs of gunshot residue should be cause for suspicion since in all likelihood the weapon was fired from a distance greater than two feet.

A final place where you should expect to find gunshot residue is on the hands of the victim, especially if the firearm was a handgun. The lack of gunpowder residue on the hands of the victim should be grounds for suspicion. If you cannot discern residue on the hands, you should "bag" the hands and discuss it with the medical examiner or coroner if either is on the scene or en route or prior to the autopsy.

In addition to entrance wounds, you may find exit wounds on the body. These types of wounds are generally larger and are more ragged then the usually neat entrance wound. As the bullet passes through the body it may turn, deflect, or shatter as it encounters tissue, organs, and bones. As it travels, the projectile will push anything in its path in front of it, which can account for the larger and irregular nature of the exit wound. There will generally be more bleeding from the exit wound than from the entrance wound for these same reasons.

Other causes for suspicion at alleged gunshot-suicide scenes would be multiple gunshot wounds, multiple shots fired, the absence of shell casings where a semiautomatic weapon was used, the questionable location of the weapon within the crime scene, the gun being held in the nondominant hand, any signs of a struggle, evidence of tissue or blood under the fingernails, or defensive-type wounds to the hands or arms of the victim. Keep in mind that not every suicidal person is successful in his or her initial attempt, and there are times when people may actually shoot themselves more than once, but this is not the norm and certainly cause for you to look further. The medical examiner may be able to tell you which wound was sustained first and if it was sufficient to cause immediate death.

If there was a close-range or contact gunshot to the head, you should expect to find the gun either in hand or within reach of the victim. If the weapon is "in hand," is it being grasped loosely or is there a *cardaveric spasm*? As described by Vernon Geberth:

> Under certain conditions, the stiffening of the hands or arms may take place immediately at the time of death. ... It is not uncommon

for persons who had a firearm or a knife in their hand at the time of death to clutch it tightly in their hands after death. ... It is impossible to "duplicate" this spasm. For example, a person attempting to place the weapon in the deceased's hand after death cannot get the same type of tight grasp."*

Aside from handguns, gunshot-suicide weapons include rifles and shotguns. The damage to the human body caused by these types of weapons is much greater, and the magnitude of disfigurement may even make physical identification impossible. Shotguns and high-velocity rifles may literally remove large portions of the head or result in large holes in the body, leaving intestines or other organs hanging out. You should expect to see more extensive burn marks and tattooing at the entrance wound with a contact or near-contact shotgun or rifle suicide. Shotgun shells are usually one of two types: rifled slugs and pellets or buckshot. When fired at contact or near contact it will be very difficult to tell these two type of shells apart since the pellets will enter the body without the opportunity to spread out; but as the distance increases from the point of impact to the barrel, the pellets will start to disperse and multiple entrance wounds will become obvious. At contact or near contact, the shotgun shell wadding will usually enter the wound directly behind the projectile(s). The lack of burn marks and tattooing at the entrance wound should be cause for suspicion, as should be a widely dispersed pattern of entrance wounds caused by shotgun pellets.

Unless the barrel of the weapon has been cut down, it is generally difficult for the suicide victim to use this long of a weapon without bringing it in direct or near-direct contact with the body. You may find that a homemade contraption such as a string or a stick was used to pull the trigger or that a toe was used. If you find such devices or that a shoe has been removed, it will lend credence to the suicide theory.

Another cause for suspicion is if the weapon (including any knife) or projectile has penetrated through the victim's clothing. Most suicide victims tend to inflict their wounds on exposed skin. If you encounter a suicide scene where the victim has been shot in the torso without first opening up his or her shirt or blouse, you should be suspicious.

If there is no weapon found at the scene, you will need to determine why before you can classify this death as a suicide. A friend or a relative may have removed it, or it could have been taken by whoever discovered the body. If the shooting occurred in a public place, the weapon may have been stolen by a passerby. Keep in mind that not all gunshot wounds cause immediate death. It is quite possible that a suicide victim who sustains a stomach or

* Vernon J. Geberth, p. 175.

chest wound could stay alive for a time after the wound is inflicted. For whatever reason, this type of victim could have disposed of or hidden the weapon him- or herself prior to death. Certainly, if it is the opinion of the medical personnel present that a single gunshot wound was sufficient to cause immediate death and no weapon is found or accounted for, you should treat this as a homicide investigation.

If the firearm is located at the scene, you will want to treat it as evidence and have it submitted for ballistic and fingerprint examination. You will want to know if the weapon is in good operating condition or if there is a malfunction of the safety mechanism if it is equipped with one. This is an important step when dealing with the possibility of an accidental discharge, either by a person who was cleaning it or by its being dropped. Horseplay with a weapon is also a possibility that should be kept in mind when interviewing family, friends, or witnesses. It is not uncommon for someone to be shot with an "unloaded" gun.

3.6 Suffocation or Hanging

About one of every five suicides is accomplished by hanging or other means of suffocation, but accidental hangings are not uncommon. Suffocation occurs when the oxygen supply is curtailed for a period of time long enough to cause death. This time frame varies from person to person but generally occurs within minutes. By far, hanging is the most common suicidal form of suffocation. Other forms can include plastic bags over the head, drowning, or any other obstruction of the airway.

Hanging usually results in a very slow and painful death. Most suicide hanging victims will jump from a piece of furniture, a ladder, or a box or attach a rope or line to a doorknob and drape it over the door etc., and will generally be suspended not too far from the ground or perhaps not suspended at all. Unlike executions by hanging or lynching, death in suicide hangings will almost always be caused by ligature strangulation, rather than by the breaking of the neck or spinal cord. The distance required to snap a person's neck during a hanging is far greater than the 2 to 3 feet or less that most hanging suicides will drop.

Suicide hanging victims will use any material available to them, such as rope, telephone or other type of wire, belts, or clothing. If the victim was alive at the time of the hanging, you should expect to see bruising around the neck, generally in the shape of an inverted V. If a fixed knot was used to tie the ligature, you should expect to see the greatest amount of bruising directly opposite where the knot is. If you see bruising or groove marks on the same side as a fixed knot, you should be suspicious. Unless the knot used was a slip-type knot, you should not expect to see bruising that is uniform around the entire neck. Uniform bruising around the neck is more consistent with homicidal ligature strangulation and should certainly be cause for suspicion. In addition to the bruising, the material used for the ligature may leave an imprint in the skin. If this imprint or groove in the skin is inconsistent with the ligature material, you should become suspicious.

Other physical changes you should expect to see in most every suffocation/hanging are petechial hemorrhages, the small red dots on the inside of the eyelids; postmortem lividity in suicide victims that have been dead for several hours, remembering that blood is subject to gravity and begins to settle in the lowest parts of the body beginning immediately after death and that this purplish staining will be permanent after 12 hours or so. You should expect to see postmortem lividity in the head of hanging victims as well, since the blood has likely been prevented from draining. Postmortem lividity in parts of the body that are inconsistent with gravity should be cause for suspicion. A swollen or bitten tongue is also a common occurrence in hangings and in strangulations in general. You may also see bleeding in and around the mouth.

At all hanging scenes you will want to safeguard the ligature material, being careful not to disturb the knot if one was used, because a forensic examination of it may produce valuable evidence or information. If you must cut the material, cut it away from the knot. One more thing about knots: There are hundreds of variations of knots, some of which require some expertise. If you encounter an unusual type of knot at a suicide scene, you should question the victim's friends and relatives regarding any special training or knowledge the victim might have had. For samples of various types of knots please visit http://www.realknots.com.

In addition to the knot, or with ligatures that did not require a knot, such as a belt, the forensics lab or medical examiner's office should examine the ligature material to learn if the victim's body weight had pulled against it. There may be skin or blood as well as stretch marks on the material.

You will also want to examine the area where the rope, line, or other material used as a ligature was secured, for it might produce forensic evidence. You will also want to examine the victim's body for signs of defensive wounds on the hands or skin or blood under the fingernails. You should also inspect the area for signs of a struggle. But keep in mind that a hanging victim may well thrash about prior to losing consciousness, possibly knocking over items in his/her immediate vicinity.

While the majority of hangings are suicides, accidental hangings are not uncommon. You may encounter infants who become entwined in pull strings from venetian blinds or other window treatments that are hanging near their cribs or whose heads become stuck between the slotted posts in their cribs, or young children who become entangled in clotheslines, etc. Adults can also accidentally become hanging victims under certain conditions. These accidents usually occur when the person is operating mechanical equipment and usually involves their clothing becoming enmeshed in the machinery.

Autoerotic hangings are also accidental rather than suicidal. *Autoerotic* refers to any sexual activity that a person participates in alone. Some people believe that a decreased oxygen supply will magnify the intensity of their orgasms, hence causing the practice of autoerotic asphyxiation. The intent is not to die but, rather, to restrict the flow of oxygen prior to and during orgasm. Hanging from a noose is one such manner of autoerotic asphyxiation; in these cases you will frequently find the body unclothed and possibly in front of a mirror. Unfortunately, this lack of oxygen sometimes results in a loss of consciousness, followed by accidental hanging. The means by which these individuals cut the air supply can be as simple as a short rope tied to a doorknob, with the person sitting against it with the noose around their heads, or they may create elaborate mechanisms that bind their arms and legs while also cutting off the oxygen supply. Some of these mechanical devices have built-in "fail-safe" devices, some of which require manual activation; however, once a person loses consciousness or becomes disoriented, these safety devices may become ineffective, hence the accidental hanging.

You may also find pornographic materials and sex toys or other objects that can be inserted into or used to manipulate erogenous zones. The majority of those persons who practice or experiment with autoerotic asphyxia are male, but often they are found to be wearing female garments or undergarments. Many teenage males also experiment with autoerotic asphyxia.

Drowning is another type of suffocation death as the water or liquid displaces the air and prevents it from getting to the lungs. Most drownings are accidental in nature and usually involve drunkenness or drugs. Suicide drownings at dwellings are rare because it is difficult for even the most determined people to keep themselves from surfacing to gasp for air. If you find a drowning victim in a bathtub, you should be suspicious, yet you should not discount an accident. You will need to carefully examine this type of victim for defensive wounds or blood or tissue under the fingernails as well as examine the entire area for additional signs of a struggle. Most drowning victims will be found floating in a larger body of water, such as a swimming pool, a lake, a river, or the ocean. Since it is so difficult to commit suicide by drowning, it is not uncommon for suicide victims to tie heavy weights to themselves to prevent them from surfacing. Unfortunately, it is not uncommon for homicide-drowning victims to be weighted down as well.

Bodies that have been in water for long periods of time will generally become unrecognizable due to the effects of putrefaction and bloating caused by this long-term submersion as well as those of sea creatures that may have been feeding on the corpse. Unless there are obvious signs that the death was caused by means other than drowning, the autopsy will usually determine the cause of death to be drowning. The autopsy may also be able to tell if the person drowned in salt water or fresh water. The presence of fresh water in a person found in the ocean will be a sign that the body had been transported to the ocean from another location.

While the autopsy may determine the cause of death to be drowning, it will be difficult for the medical examiner of coroner to determine if the death was suicide, accidental, or homicidal. The totality of the investigation may or may not reveal a mode of death, but as the investigator you will need to make every effort to pursue this goal. Once the victim has been positively identified by relatives or through fingerprint or dental examination, the investigator will be able to determine if the person had been reported missing. If so, a fairly extensive investigation may already have been conducted into the circumstances of the disappearance. A search of the victim's residence and place of employment should be conducted for suicide notes, signs of depression, or signs of foul play. These searches must be accomplished within the scope of the applicable state or federal laws. As with any other suicide investigation, interviews of relatives, friends, and coworkers and canvass of neighbors will need to be conducted, and the victim's medical history will need to be reviewed for signs of emotional distress, life-altering events that would lead to depression, etc.

3.7 Knives and Stab Wounds

While not the most popular means of suicide, cutting and/or stabbing oneself to death is a common enough method among suicidal individuals. The availability of cutting and stabbing instruments is far greater than that of firearms. One need only open a kitchen drawer or medicine cabinet to find the means necessary to take one's life, yet knives, razors, ice picks, and similar tools generally do not provide the immediate result that a firearm will. Suicide victims who cut or stab themselves will generally remain conscious and possibly mobile for a period of time after inflicting the wound or wounds; and if they are discovered by another person prior to their death they may even survive what would otherwise have been a fatal wound. Keep in mind that this type of victim may have moved about considerably after inflicting these types of wounds, so you may observe a scene in which furniture is overturned or blood evidence is in various places throughout the area.

The stereotypical suicide by this type of instrument involves the slashing of the wrists, and it is not uncommon to see several parallel slashes in the same immediate area. These additional cuts can be considered hesitation wounds inflicted prior to the wound that was sufficient to cause severe bleeding. These hesitation wounds will generally be more superficial in nature as the suicide victim realizes that he/she did not use enough strength to achieve the desired result.

Another typical suicide wound will be the self-inflicted wound to the throat. This too will generally be a slashing or cutting-type wound that may sever the carotid artery or a major blood vessel.

The stabbing-suicide victim will usually have a wound to the chest in an attempt to pierce the heart. As with the hesitation wounds that are common with wrist slashing, suicidal stabbers may inflict several wounds in the same general area. These additional wounds will usually be shallow penetrations as the person's resolve is tested or the strength necessary to puncture the chest cavity is determined.

While most suicide stab wounds are to the chest, some suicide victims will disfigure other parts of their bodies or disembowel themselves, giving the impression that their death may have been a ritualistic homicide. Again, you must take the totality of the evidence into consideration. Is the weapon present? Is there a suicide note? Was there depression or life-altering events? Were suicidal intentions voiced by the deceased prior to the act?

Chopping wounds are usually large gaping wounds caused by heavy instruments such as axes, machetes, picks, and shovels. This type of wound is rarely associated with suicide and therefore should be considered suspicious. Wounds of this nature are usually found around the head and shoulders as well as defensive wounds to the arms and hands.

You should be suspicious at alleged suicidal slashing/stabbing scenes if the weapon is not present; if the wounds were made through the victim's clothing rather than directly to the skin; if you observe defensive wounds or cuts to the palms, forearms, or knuckles of the victim; if there are multiple wounds that all appear to be deep rather than varying in depth; if there are wounds to multiple parts of the body or that would be difficult or impossible to reach; if there are crisscrossed cuts; etc.

3.8 Poisons/Overdoses

Merriam-Webster's Online Dictionary describes poison as:

> **1 a :** a substance that through its chemical action usually kills, injures, or impairs an organism **b** (1) **:** something destructive or harmful (2) **:** an object of aversion or abhorrence
>
> **2 :** a substance that inhibits the activity of another substance or the course of a reaction or process <a catalyst *poison*>*

This definition does not begin to quantify the number of potential poisons available to the average person. These substances can be solids, liquids, or gases, and they may be found in common everyday products such as cleaning solutions, in over-the-counter or prescription medications, occurring naturally in plant life, used in manufacturing processes, as a result of animal bites, etc.

If there are no overt indications as to the cause or mode of death at the scene, such as a suicide note, empty or near-empty pill bottles, caustic chemicals, syringes, or a witness, the death may appear to be of natural causes and you will probably not know that a poison or overdose was involved until the completion of the autopsy. While suicide deaths by poisoning or overdose are common, the absence of a suicide note or other evidence indicating self-ingestion should be cause for suspicion.

If there is evidence at the scene such as pills, empty pill capsules, and chemicals, it should be collected and safeguarded in accordance with good crime scene procedures. The coroner who will perform the autopsy should be made aware of this evidence, which will assist him or her in ordering toxicological tests and in comparing them to the evidence sample.

If you are notified that a death was not natural but due to poisoning, the coroner should be able to tell you what the poison was, that is, chemical/pharmaceutical, organic, gaseous, etc. It is now your responsibility to determine the source. If the scene is still being safeguarded, a complete crime scene search and investigation should be conducted. If the scene is no longer under your control, you will need to obtain permission from an authorized person or obtain a search warrant. Again, every effort must be made to comply with the laws that govern your area.

Soiled glasses, bottles, plates, silverware, food containers, pots and pans, or any other vessel used to contain or consume food or drink should be collected. All medicines and hypodermic needles as well as any caustic chemicals should be collected. Where possible, food and liquid samples should be retrieved from the garbage, sinks, and plumbing. Friends, neighbors, and coworkers should be interviewed to determine if the victim had shown any suicidal signs or had experienced any life-alerting events. The victim's papers, personal belongings, writings, phone records, and phone answering machine should be safeguarded and reviewed. A recent timeline should be established for the victim so that his/her activities and places visited can be identified.

Most suicide poisoning victims will use a poison or product with which they are familiar. Very rarely will someone ingest curare or coral snake venom. If you are unable to determine the source at the scene or are faced with a rare or exotic poison, you should take into consideration the victim's type

---

* *Merriam-Webster's Online Dictionary*: http://www.m-w.com/cgi-bin/dictionary

of employment, both past and present, as well as hobbies and educational background to develop potential leads. You must consider not only suicide or homicide when dealing with poisonings; you must also consider accidental poisoning or overdose as well.

3.9 Deaths at Fire Scenes

In 2001, there were 3,309 accidental deaths attributed to exposure to smoke, fire, and flames.*

In addition, there were 76 deaths of this nature that could not be classified as an accident, a suicide, or a homicide and are listed by the National Safety Counsel as an "event of undetermined intent." While rare in our society, self-immolation or suicide by fire does occur in the United States and cannot be discounted.

Unlike most other death scenes, a fire-death scene is usually not under the direct control of the police. While the fire is actively being fought, the police are there to provide security and to control onlookers and traffic. Once the fire is extinguished, it is usually a firefighter who will discover a body or bodies. As with any other death scene, the safety of everyone present should be the first concern; but the scene should be secured pending the arrival of the medical examiner or coroner and investigators.

While some police departments have trained arson investigators, this type of scene is usually the domain of the Fire Department. In all suspicious fires and all fires that involve death(s), an arson investigation should be conducted to determine the cause and origin of the fire. Arson investigation is a highly specialized field requiring training that is not available to the average investigator or crime scene technician. The arson investigator will be trained in the collection and handling of evidence, and he/she should be in charge of the scene until the completion of his or her investigation. If the arson investigator determines that the cause of the fire was accidental, the police department's only concern should be the safety of the scene, the identification of the victims, and notification of next of kin.

On the other hand, if the determination is arson, a complete homicide investigation should be conducted. At this stage the police department should assume responsibility for follow-up investigation. While arson investigators have specialized knowledge in fire cause and origin, they will not possess the expertise, tools, local knowledge, or experience of homicide investigators.

---

* *Source*: National Safety Council estimates based on data from National Center for Health Statistics and U.S. Census Bureau

As a police or fire investigator you would do well to establish a rapport with your counterparts in your area. Cooperation and the sharing of knowledge will assist both investigators and their respective departments in accomplishing their missions.

As discussed earlier, there are four reasons that people die: (1) from natural causes (including diseases), (2) accidentally (including natural disasters), (3) suicide, and (4) homicide. If the death investigation, including that of the medical examiner or coroner, concludes that death was as a result one of the first three reasons, no further police investigation will usually be required, unless the victim(s) remains unidentified. Identification of victims is discussed in Chapter 4, "Homicide Investigations."

Homicide Investigations

4

Each law enforcement agency will have rules and procedures for conducting homicide or for that matter any type of criminal investigation. If you work in a large metropolitan area there will likely be a team of investigators, headed by a detective supervisor assigned to the initial investigation, and a crime scene unit to process and collect evidence. If you work as an investigator for a smaller department, you may be the only investigator assigned to the case.

This section begins with the premise that deaths by natural causes, accident, or suicide have been eliminated and it has been established that a murder or murders have been committed. It is also assumed that the first officer(s) have followed good crime scene procedures and have secured the area, provided first aid if there were any signs of life, obtained a dying declaration if the victim was still conscious upon the officers' arrival, arrested the perpetrator if possible, detained and segregated witnesses and suspects, and taken good notes.

The final assumptions of this section are that the crime scene search has been completed in accordance with the procedures described in this book, the writings of Dr. Henry Lee, and Vernon Geberth; the scene has been processed and released, and you are aware of the results of forensic examinations of the collected evidence; the initial canvass for witnesses has been completed; and the body has been autopsied and you are aware of the results.

If you are responding to the scene from your office, you should take the time to make sure you have everything you will need. Bring pens, pencils with erasers, new steno pads, graph paper, a commercially available homicide investigation kit if one is supplied by your department or a kit of your own making as previously described, Polaroid and conventional or digital camera with ample film (both black-and-white and color) or storage medium for the digital camera, a video camera, police radios, a tape recorder with several unopened cassette tapes, and a cellular telephone. For outdoor scenes, you will need to consider appropriate clothing, lighting, shelter, safety issues, and communications issues.

If you are responding from a remote location, you should arrange for others to bring the appropriate items to the scene for you.

4.1 Identity of the Victim

Murder investigations involve a double "who" to accompany the "why, what, where, when, and how." The first "who" that needs to be answered is the identity of the victim, the second being the identity of the perpetrator. In the vast majority of homicides, the tentative identity of the victim is readily known, from either relatives or friends at the scene or from personal identification on the victim's body. In these cases, these friends or relatives will usually make a positive identification to the coroner or medical examiner prior to the autopsy. Sometimes, however, the identity of the victim may not be known, because of either disfigurement, dismemberment, decomposition, or a lack of identifying documents, friends, or relatives. The importance of knowing who the victim is cannot be overstated. For example, a stabbing victim found on the side of a quiet country road with no personal identification on their person would leave nowhere to go to locate relatives, friends, coworkers, or the victim's residence, vehicle, etc. Sure, there may be other evidence, such as tire marks, footmarks, and blood, at the scene, but the bulk of the investigation will begin, perhaps even leading to an additional crime scene or two, once the victim has been identified.

The most obvious means of identification in the absence of relatives, friends, or documentation is through the use of fingerprints, assuming of course that it is possible to obtain prints from the victim and that there are prints on file to compare them with. Other means include checking missing persons reports, publishing photographs, physical description, (including tattoos, scars, jewelry, etc.), use of dentistry, DNA, and facial reconstructions by a forensic anthropologist. For a thorough review of identification techniques for unknown murder victims, investigators are advised to read *Practical Homicide Investigation* by Vernon Geberth.

4.2 Arrests at the Scene

In cases where a perpetrator has been arrested at or near the scene by patrol officers, you should interview the officers and any witnesses at the scene to gain an understanding of the probable cause that led to the arrest. You will need to know if the arrestee had made any spontaneous statements or voluntary statements to the officer or any nonpolice third party and if the officer has advised him of his Miranda rights.

If you learn that the arrestee has made statements or is talkative and cooperative, you should seize this opportunity to conduct an interrogation utilizing videotape or audiotape rather than waiting to conduct the interrogation at the police station or prosecutor's office. Prior to conducting this interview, you should become completely familiar with the crime scene and the nature of the homicide. You should read the Miranda warnings to the subject, rather than attempting to recite them from memory, and, if conditions allow, the subject should be interviewed in a relaxed atmosphere, without being restrained by handcuffs and with no more than one other law enforcement officer present. The object is to conduct this interrogation while the arrestee is cooperative and without the appearance of threat or intimidation.

If you learn that that the arrestee has not been cooperative at the scene, you should arrange to conduct the video or audio interrogation at the police station or prosecutor's office. Typically, these interrogations occur hours after the homicide and initial arrest, during which interim the defendant has had an opportunity to prepare himself/herself. It is the duty of the investigator to be better prepared, have a complete knowledge of the crime scene, victimology, defendant's history, and good interrogation technique.

Remember, the arrest of a suspect at or near the scene, with or without a confession, does not negate the need for a proper and thorough crime scene search and a complete investigation, including the canvass, processing of the crime scene for evidence, witness interviews, etc.

You should also determine where the arrestee has been kept since being taken into custody, e.g., the back seat of a police car, a room within a house, or a backyard, so that the immediate area can be searched for evidence. You should examine the arrestee's clothing, hands, hair, etc., for signs of blood, cuts, bruising, or other types of transferable evidence. You should ensure that the arrestee has been removed from view of the crime scene and away from contact with any witnesses. Once the initial interrogation has been completed, or if no interrogation will be conducted at the scene, the perpetrator should be transported to the detective unit office and kept under observation at all times to prevent him/her from washing up or disposing of any possible evidence. This includes escorting and observing the arrestee in the event that he/she requires going to the bathroom.

A word about videotaping custodial interrogations: As of June 2004, the states of Alaska, Illinois, Minnesota, and Maine have enacted laws mandating the videotaping of custodial interrogations conducted at law enforcement facilities, and new laws are being proposed in other states throughout the country. Additionally, many local municipalities, police departments, and prosecutor's offices around the country have instituted or are instituting their own policies to require the videotaping of custodial interrogations. While some in the law enforcement community believe this requirement to be yet another obstacle to the successful investigation of crime and prosecution of defendants, proponents of videotaping have produced convincing evidence to the contrary. One thing is certain: The production of a videotaped interrogation at trial will all but eliminate the claims of defendants that they were not given their Miranda rights, that their confession was coerced, that they asked to speak to their lawyer but were ignored, or that the police are lying about what they said. The real obstacle that has been placed in the way of law enforcement has been the requirement to inform everyone in a custodial interrogation of his or her Miranda rights. If the defendant is willing to answer questions after being advised of these rights, videotaping of the entire interrogation can only benefit the law enforcement community.

4.3 No Arrest at the Scene

What remains of the investigation can be broken down into three sections: (1) evaluation of the physical evidence and test results, including comparisons to known cases of a similar nature, (2) evaluation and continued investigation of eyewitnesses, continued canvass, and victim profile, and (3) arrest or closing of the active investigation.

4.4 Evaluation and Pursuit of Evidence

The physical evidence and subsequent test results will vary from case to case. As the investigator, you will need to depend on the expertise of the coroner/medical examiner, crime scene technicians, police lab, and other specialists, such as forensic dentists, anthropologists, and handwriting experts. None of these individuals, you included, should act in a vacuum. Good communication among all involved in a murder investigation is essential. As stated by Vernon Geberth, "The criminal investigator should be aware of the contributions forensic experts, such as forensic anthropologists and dentists, can lend to the process. ... I recommend that the homicide investigator establish personal contact with these forensic people and include them in the investigative team"* By using such experts as odontologists you may be able to learn the perpetrator's approximate age, height, socioeconomic status, blood type, and perhaps even sexual preference, all from a bite mark on the victim's body.

* *Practical Homicide Investigation*, 2nd ed., p. 191.

In cases where the victim's face has been mutilated, disfigured, decomposed, or the like, a forensic anthropologist may be able to reconstruct it with great accuracy, and a forensic examination of the victim's remains, no matter how little is recovered, may provide their height, weight, race, sex, and perhaps even a positive identification by comparison to known dental records.

Medical examiners often rely on nonmedical information given to them by detectives to explain unexpected or contradictory findings, and the medical examiner can frequently provide the detective with information regarding the height or strength or sometimes even whether the perpetrator is right- or left-handed. Fingerprints, DNA, ballistics, blood, tools and tool marks, handwritten, typed, or computer-generated printed material, computer drives, etc., are all areas that will require an expertise that is usually beyond the capabilities of the average professional investigator. You should seek the assistance of these and other experts and engage in a give-and-take with them as the investigation continues.

4.5 Evaluation of Victim and Witnesses

After the initial crime scene investigation has been completed, a thorough review of all the information gathered is essential for the organization of the known facts. If you are the only investigator assigned to this case, you will not have far to look. On the other hand, if you are assisted by a team of detectives, some of whom have been interviewing witnesses while others have been conducting a canvass or processing the crime scene, you will have a lot of coordinating and collating to do. Many police departments have purchased or developed relational database programs to assist investigators in organizing complex investigations. Yet some departments still utilize paper or index card systems to list information on witnesses, vehicles, property, evidence, etc. Whatever the method, it is recommended that a complete review or critique be conducted after the initial investigation has been completed so that the future direction of the case may be determined. This can ensure that anyone missed during the initial canvass is located and interviewed and help determine which interviews or reinterviews of the victim's associates, friends, relatives, and acquaintances remain to be done. A complete background check of these individuals should be conducted and, if necessary, compared to the known information that has been developed so far. Remember, everyone is a suspect until you can eliminate him or her.

Since everyone is considered a suspect, do you need to provide Miranda warnings before conducting interviews? No, police are required to issue Miranda warnings only when two simultaneous things occur: (1) The person being questioned is in police custody and no longer free to leave, and (2) an interrogation is about to occur. The investigator must take care to avoid giving the perception that the person being interviewed is not free to leave if he or she is. The line between interviewing and interrogation is simply the manner in which questions are asked. "Were you ever in St. Louis?" is not interrogation, but "Were you at 300 Kennedy Boulevard in St. Louis last Wednesday afternoon at 2:15 P.M.?" is an interrogation question. Miranda warnings are not necessary prior to interrogation-type questions as long as the person is not in custody or made to feel as if he or she is in custody.

When conducting interviews of witnesses, friends, relatives, coworkers, and acquaintances, you will be looking to learn everything they know about the victim, about the relationships with other people the victim knew, and about the person being interviewed as well. Everyone is a suspect, yet your initial interviews should be cordial fact-finding missions rather than accusatory. The focus should remain on the victim, yet you should be listening for and gathering information on every person interviewed.

A review of the victim's personal papers, telephone calls, mail, computer, and other such documents belonging to the victim will need to be conducted, as will a continued in-depth investigation of the victim's personal, medical, and professional life. Depending on the circumstances in each case, you may require a court-ordered search warrant to obtain certain items, especially records or information that are under the control of or that directly affect third parties. It is by conducting this type of victimology that motive and opportunity may be discovered.

As with the team concept for medical and forensic experts discussed earlier, a close working relationship and understanding of each other's responsibilities should be developed with the prosecutor's office. The prosecutor can provide you with the legal resources that may be required to obtain search warrants and court-ordered wiretaps and surveillances and to guide you around the many pitfalls within the criminal justice system. Keep in mind, however, that the prosecutor views your investigation with an eye to proving the case *beyond a reasonable doubt*. This standard is far greater than the one imposed by law on the police: *probable cause*.

As an investigator you should strive to collect, deduce, and compile evidence that can satisfy the prosecutor's quest for proof beyond a reasonable doubt, yet the law realizes that this is not always possible. So what is probable cause? The Bill of Rights makes mention of it in Amendment IV:

> IV: The right of the people to be secure in their persons, houses, papers, and effects, against unreasonable searches and seizures, shall not be violated, and no Warrants shall issue, but upon probable cause supported by oath or affirmation, and particularly describing the place to be searched, and the persons or things to be seized.*

But this is not a definition of probable cause, only an acknowledgment that it exists. Many definitions exist for this elusive theory, and the concept has been tested in the courts throughout our history. Two words keep appearing in almost every court decision: *reasonable* and *prudent*. If your investigation has produced evidence that would make an average reasonable and prudent (or cautious) person believe that a crime has been committed or is being committed or, in the case of obtaining a search warrant, that the contraband or evidence actually exists in the place you wish to search, then you have established probable cause. This evidence or information can come from your crime scene, autopsy, witnesses, suspects, circumstantial evidence, and situations such as exclusive opportunity. So long as you act in a reasonable and prudent fashion and in good will, the courts will usually uphold your findings of probable cause.

4.6 Who Commits Murder, and Where?

The following chart, from the U.S. Department of Justice, Bureau of Statistics report on "Homicide trends in the U.S.," indicates that the highest percentage of homicides occur in large cities (Figure 4-1).

Certain Homicide Types Vary by Size of Place

For the years 1976–2000 combined, large cities were much more commonly the site of drug-related and gang-related killings and relatively less likely to be the location of family-related and work-related homicides.

Homicide Type by Urbanicity, 1976–2000

	Percent of All Homicides			
	Large City	Small City	Suburban	Rural
All homicides	57.3%	11.4%	20.9%	10.5%

The Proportion of Homicides That Are Intimate Homicides Differs by Type of Area

The greatest decline in intimate murders occurred in large cities. From 1976 to 2000, the number of intimate murders in large cities fell by more than half, while nonintimate murders increased in

˙ The United States Bill of Rights. The Ten Original Amendments to the Constitution of the United States Passed by Congress September 25, 1789, Ratified December 15, 1791.

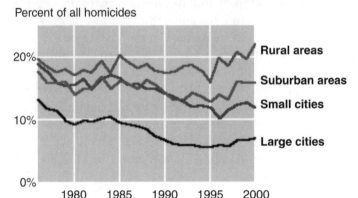

Percent of all homicides involving inmates by urban, suburban, and rural area, 1976-2000

Percent of all homicides

Figure 4-1

the late 1980s and 1990s but fell after 1993, in small cities dropped by over 46%, although nonintimate homicides showed little change in rural areas dropped by 36%, less than the 44% drop in nonintimate homicides in suburban areas declined by 31%, exceeding the 22% drop in nonintimate homicides. Intimate homicides made up a larger proportion of murders in rural areas than in suburban or urban areas. Note: Large cities have a population of 100,000 or more, while small cities have populations of fewer than 100,000.

Here's another interesting statistic provided by the DOJ:

For murder victims, 43% were related to or acquainted with their assailants, 14% of victims were murdered by strangers, while 43% of victims had an unknown relationships to their murderers in 2002.[*]

While the DOJ statistics also indicate dramatic increases in drug- and gang-related murders during 1996–2000, the majority of the victims were killed by someone they knew, while only 14% were killed by confirmed strangers. The DOJ breaks these numbers down further by indicating that "family members were most likely to murder a young child — about one in five child murders was committed by a family member — while a friend or acquaintance was most likely to murder an older child age 15 to 17."[†]

It is clear that in many instances the murderer and the victim will know each other, either intimately as family, former family, boyfriend/girlfriend,

---

[*] USDOJ, Bureau of Statistics, *Crime Characteristics.*
[†] USDOJ, Bureau of Statistics, *Crime Characteristics.*

coworkers, neighbors, competitors, gang members, or other more casual relationships. Every investigator should be aware of these general statistics, and a complete review of the DOJ reports is recommended. But by no means should these statistics give you a predisposition. As the investigator, you must approach every case with an open mind and a blank list of suspects.

4.7 Suspect List

At some point in time you will have identified and interviewed all of the victim's known relatives and acquaintances, both friend and foe, learned the victim's habits, likes, dislikes, hobbies, sexual preferences, physical and mental health issues, education, interests, finances, and more. You will also have constructed a timeline of the victim's activities going backwards as far as possible, learning whom the victim was with and where. You now have the means to construct a listing of all suspects, eliminating those with obvious and confirmed alibis.

4.8 Motive, Means, Opportunity

As your investigation continues, you should begin to develop one or more theories about your case. Why would someone murder your victim? Were the victim and murderer known to each other? family members? Was this a stalking case? a serial murder? gang or drug related? When exploring motives you should keep in mind the most common ones: passion, anger, hatred, envy, revenge, fear, and profit. With these motives in mind, you can review them against your suspect list and the information you have developed from their interviews. If you identify persons with motives, you will need to follow up with further investigation, including additional interviews with them, their associates, their employers, etc.

The means or ability to commit murder will vary from person to person and from case to case. Did this murder require any special skill, strength, technical knowledge, or expertise? The information you have learned from the crime scene and forensic investigation should be taken into consideration when trying to determine if the suspects had the means or ability to commit the crime. While certainly not definitive, investigators should be aware that men and women statistically use different types of weapons. According the DOJ, "Male offenders were more likely than female offenders (28% to 15%) to have used a weapon such as a blunt object knife or firearm in the commission of the violent offense."[*]

---

[*] USDOJ, Office of Justice Programs, *Women Offenders* (Dec. 1999, Revised 10/3/2000), p, 3.

This same report goes on to say that "Just over half of women committing murder and two-thirds of males committing murder used a firearm. Female offenders were substantially more likely than male murderers to have used a knife or other sharp object to commit the crime."

People Without the Means to Commit the Murder Should Be Moved Down the List

You should be attempting to construct a timeline for each suspect to see if and when it crosses that of the victim. Suspects who have not had an obvious opportunity to commit the murder should be moved down the list, and you should focus on those who had been with or near the victim and those whom you have been unable to time track.

This process of elimination works well in cases where the victim and perpetrator were known to each other. You may find that a limited number of suspects had motive, means, and opportunity to commit the murder. But what about nonrelational murders?

4.9 Serial Killers, Sexual Homicides, and Random Murders

As discussed earlier, the majority of homicide victims knew their killers. Yet how can you investigate murders committed by strangers? Most investigators will not encounter a Son of Sam, a Ted Bundy, a Jeffrey Dahmer, or a John Wayne Gacy throughout their careers, yet there are predators such as these in every society. Anatoly Onoprienko was responsible for at least 50 murders in Ukraine, while Jack the Ripper murdered only five prostitutes in London during the late 1800s.

Without the proper reporting, analysis, dissemination, and accessibility of information locally, regionally, and nationally, the identification of a pattern or serial killer would come to light only by coincidence. Good communication among local, state, and federal law enforcement agencies is indispensable in this regard.

The obvious agency of choice to fill this need at the national level was and is the FBI.

National Center for the Analysis of Violent Crime

"The mission of the National Center for the Analysis of Violent Crime (NCAVC) is to combine investigative and operational support functions, research, and training in order to provide assistance, without charge, to federal, state, local, and foreign law enforcement agencies investigating unusual or repetitive violent crimes."[*]

There are three investigative analysis units within NCAVC: CASMIRC, VICAP, and BAU.

CASMIRC

The Morgan P. Hardiman Child Abduction and Serial Murder Investigative Resources Center (CASMIRC) was established as part of Public Law 105-314, the Protection of Children From Sexual Predators Act, passed by Congress on October 30, 1998. The legislation provides that the U.S. Attorney General shall establish within the FBI's NCAVC a CASMIRC in order to provide investigative support through the coordination and provision of federal law enforcement resources, training, and application of other multidisciplinary expertise and to assist federal, state, and local authorities in matters involving child abductions, mysterious disappearances of children, child homicide, and serial murder across the country. Therefore, the overall strategic goal of CASMIRC, as set forth in the legislation, is to reduce the impact of these crimes.*

This investigative program is designed to assist local, state, and federal law enforcement agencies in the identification of investigation of violent pattern criminals and predators who prey on children.

Violent Criminal Apprehension Program (ViCAP)

ViCAP's mission is to facilitate cooperation, communication, and coordination between law enforcement agencies and to provide support in their efforts to investigate, identify, track, apprehend, and prosecute violent serial offenders. ViCAP is a nationwide data information center designed to collect, collate, and analyze crimes of violence, specifically murder. Cases meeting the ViCAP submission criteria with an arrested or identified offender can be entered into the ViCAP system by law enforcement investigators for database comparison and possible matching with unsolved cases. Additionally, criteria cases with an unidentified offender may be submitted for database comparison.

Once a case is entered into the ViCAP database, it is compared continually against all other entries on the basis of certain aspects of the crime. The purpose of this process is to detect signature aspects/traits of homicide and similar patterns of modus operandi (MOs), which will in turn allow ViCAP personnel to pinpoint those crimes that have been committed by the same offender. When pat-

---

* FBI: http://www.fbi.gov/hq/isd/cirg/ncavc.htm
* FBI: http://www.fbi.gov/hq/isd/cirg/ncavc.htm

terns are found, involved law enforcement agencies will be notified
of the results and they will pursue the information for lead value.[*]

Behavioral Analysis Unit (BAU) — East/West Regions

The mission of the BAU is to provide behavioral-based investigative
and operational support by applying case experience, research, and
training to complex and time-sensitive crimes, typically involving
acts or threats of violence. … BAU assistance to law enforcement
agencies is provided through the process of "criminal investigative
analysis." Criminal investigative analysis is a process of reviewing
crimes from both a behavioral and investigative perspective. It involves reviewing and assessing the facts of a criminal act, interpreting
offender behavior, and interaction with the victim, as exhibited during the commission of the crime or as displayed in the crime scene.
BAU staff conduct detailed analyses of crimes for the purpose of
providing one or more of the following services: crime analysis,
investigative suggestions, profiles of unknown offenders, threat analysis, critical incident analysis, interview strategies, major case management, search warrant assistance, prosecutive and trial strategies,
and expert testimony.[†]

How do you determine if the case you are investigating may be part of
a larger pattern, perhaps one that spans the entire country or beyond? The
totality of your investigation, including witnesses, physical and forensic evidence, victimology, mode of death, etc., should provide you with a theory.
If your theory is that the murder was a relational one, you should pursue
that angle. On the other hand, if there is no indication that the victim may
have known the killer, or if your victim remains unidentified, or if there are
signs of extraordinary wounds, bite marks, eviscerations, postmortem posing
of the body, missing body parts, missing jewelry, unknown writing at the
scene, or contact through the media or directly to law enforcement, you
should contact the FBI and request their assistance.

Unfortunately, not every mystery gets reported to the FBI, so in addition
you should contact neighboring precincts, adjoining municipalities, and city,
county, and state police regarding cases of a similar nature.

4.10 Closing Homicide Investigations

Solvability

According to the FBI's national crime statistics for *Homicide Trends in the
United States:*

---

[*] FBI, http://www.fbi.gov/hq/isd/cirg/ncavc.htm
[†] FBI, http://www.fbi.gov/hq/isd/cirg/ncavc.htm

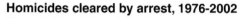

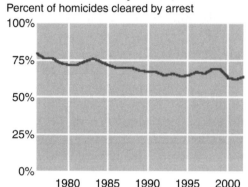

Homicides cleared by arrest, 1976-2002
Percent of homicides cleared by arrest

Figure 4-2

- The percentage of homicides cleared by arrest has been declining.
- In 2002, 64% of all homicides were cleared, compared to 79% in 1976.
- Homicide has the highest clearance rate of all serious crimes.*

As seen in the Figure 4-2, the clearance rate for homicide has been on the decline in the United States since 1976. One theory for this has been the increasing numbers of homicides committed in connection with drug usage and/or trafficking by individuals and by organized crime. In this context the term *organized crime* is used to describe any and all groups of individuals that act for a criminal purpose, including South and Central American, Caribbean, Asian, and European drug cartels as well as the Mafia. Some of these drug-related homicides are well-orchestrated "hits" by professional assassins, while others are the result of "turf" rivalries or drive-by shootings.

While this trend is troubling, it is not unstoppable. The professional investigators should avail themselves of all useful intelligence from local, state, and federal drug enforcement agencies. Much of the information obtained by these departments comes from the use of confidential informants, who in addition to narcotics trafficking may have information on drug-related murders.

The use of confidential informants is also common among non-drug-related investigators and police officers, and their sources of information can also assist you in a homicide investigation. Murders have been and will continue to be committed by burglars, robbers, sexual predators, con artists, etc.

In addition to homicides that are cleared by arrests, some homicides can be cleared by *exceptional means*: "Law enforcement agencies clear or solve an offense when at least one person is arrested, charged with the commission

---

* U.S. Department of Justice, Office of Justice Programs, *Bureau of Justice Statistics: Homicide Trends in the U.S.*

of the offense, and turned over to the court for prosecution. Law enforcement agencies may also clear a crime by exceptional means, such as when an identified offender is killed during apprehension or commits suicide."* Additional exceptional means of clearance occur when an identified offender has died of any means, be it natural or homicidal, or when he or she has been incarcerated on other charges and for whatever legal reason will not be returned to your jurisdiction for prosecution.

The National Institute for Justice conducted extensive research into the solvability of homicides and concluded that the way in which a homicide case is investigated will have a direct effect on the outcome. This study was published as the *NIJ Journal*, no. 243, in April 2000 and lists the following factors as having a positive effect on solvability:

Factors within Police Control That Lead to Closure

Initial Response:

• The first officer on the scene immediately notifies the homicide unit, medical examiner's office, and crime lab.

• The first officer on the scene secures the area and attempts to locate witnesses.

• A detective arrives at the scene within 30 minutes.

Actions of Detectives:

• Three or four detectives are assigned to the case.

• Detectives describe the crime scene, including measurements, in their notes.

• Detectives follow up on all witness information.

• Detectives attend the postmortem examination.

Other Police Responses:

• A computer check, using the local Criminal Justice Information System, is conducted on the suspect, the gun, and any witnesses.

---

* U.S. Department of Justice, Office of Justice Programs, *Bureau of Justice Statistics: Homicide Trends in the U.S.*

• A witness at the crime scene provides valuable information about the circumstances of the death, the motivation, the identification of the suspect, or victim, and the whereabouts of the suspect.

• Witnesses, friends, acquaintances, and neighbors of the victim are interviewed.

• The medical examiner prepares a body chart of the victim.

• The attending physician and medical personnel are interviewed.

• Confidential informants are used.[*]

This report goes on to conclude:

The probability of clearance increases significantly when the first officer on the scene quickly notifies the homicide unit, the medical examiners, and the crime lab and attempts to locate witnesses, secure the area, and identify potential witnesses in the neighborhood.

The data indicate that the number of detectives assigned to a case is particularly important: Assigning a minimum of three detectives and perhaps four appears to increase the likelihood of clearing it. Assigning more than four detectives does not appear to make a difference unless an agency makes a massive investment of 11 or more detectives. Only one city, which had a high homicide clearance rate, routinely used a great number of homicide detectives on a case. That city used 11 detectives in 63% of the 200 cases in its sample.[†]

So it is apparent that not all homicide investigations are created equally and that the policies of the investigating agency have a direct impact on the solvability of these types of investigations.

4.11 Arrests in Homicide Investigations

In a perfect world all homicide investigations would result in the arrest and conviction of the murderer. Ours is not a perfect world. History has shown

[*] Criminal justice system, *NIJ Journal* 243, April 2000.
[†] Criminal justice system, *NIJ Journal* 243, April 2000.

us that not every homicide case is solved, not every arrested murderer gets convicted, and not all convicted murderers are guilty. Certainly, some of these problems are the result of undertrained or inexperienced investigators, while at other times even the most skilled investigators will fail. Your obligation as a professional investigator is to provide the most thorough, complete, and competent investigation possible. Good investigators will show a dogged determination to follow through until every avenue of investigation has been exhausted. Often this may require multiple interviews of witnesses and or suspects, extensive background research into the victim and his or her relationships, review of existing evidence, and comparison to other similar cases. Good evidence gathering, handling, and safeguarding are essential, as is proper and precise reporting and documentation so that your work will be sustained at a trial.

While "probable cause" may be the legal requirement to support an arrest, every investigator should strive for the indisputable evidence that the person being arrested is indeed the perpetrator. Great care must be taken at every step of the investigation to ensure that all of the evidence uncovered is done in such a way as to withstand challenges under the "exclusionary rule" derived from the Fourth Amendment to the U.S. Constitution, which prohibits evidence that is seized illegally from being used against a defendant at trial. (see *Mapp v. Ohio*)*

As a professional investigator you should keep in mind that you will not have an opportunity to give a narration of your investigative findings to a jury; rather, your information will find its way into the court in a piecemeal fashion. The prosecutor will attempt to introduce evidence from you and others, while the defense will take every opportunity to oppose it, minimize it, or discredit it. Many times, for one reason or another, the information you possess and that in your mind seals the guilt of the defendant may never reach the jury.

Know the laws relating to evidence, know the laws relating to custodial interrogation, and seek legal advice from the prosecutor's office or your own department's legal bureau whenever you have any doubts.

* Mapp v. Ohio, U.S. 643 (1961).

Interrogations and Confessions

5

Interrogations, or the direct questioning of a subject for the purpose of obtaining a confession, can take place before or after an arrest. As stated earlier, interrogations of persons not in custody do not require Miranda warnings. Again, a person is in custody when he/she is not free to leave or believes that he/she is not free to leave. If a person is in the back seat of a police vehicle, seated between two law enforcement officials, he will probably be able to demonstrate to the court that he had reason to believe he/she was not free to leave. The best interrogator may have confessions suppressed under this type of circumstance. You have no obligation to tell your suspects that they are free to leave, but you do have the obligation not to intentionally make them feel like they cannot. While you cannot control what goes on in the minds of others, the court will view your actions in terms of your intent or good will. If the court believes that your intent was to make the defendant feel as if he was in custody, then whatever confession you do obtain may be suppressed without first reading Miranda warnings to the defendant.

On the other hand, if this interrogation is taking place after an arrest, Miranda warnings must be read to the defendant and his/her consent obtained prior to the beginning of the interrogation. At this point the interrogator may be able to use the defendant's loss of freedom to the interrogator's advantage. When does an arrest occur? Again, it occurs at the first moment that the person is deprived of the freedom to leave.

5.1 Interrogation Warning: Absolute Right to Counsel

Other important aspects you must be aware of before interrogating prisoners relate to arrest warrants, accusatory instruments, the defendant's representation by counsel on unrelated charges, and a defendant's absolute right to counsel before being questioned. Again, the laws of your state as well as federal law will have an effect on this absolute right and when it becomes effective. For example, regarding filing of accusatory instruments before arrest:

> It is well settled that under both the federal and state constitutions, the right to counsel attaches upon the commencement of criminal proceedings. In New York, however, CPL 120.20 requires an accusatory instrument to be filed before an arrest warrant may issue. Thus the indelible right to counsel attaches when an arrest warrant issues (see *People v. Harris*, 77 N.Y.2d 434, 440 [1991]).*

Each state's laws will deal with this issue in its own way. But one thing is certain: You will not be able to question a defendant without his or her lawyer being present once this "accusatory instrument" is filed in whatever form your state requires.

5.2 The Need for Arrest Warrants

A source of major concern for law enforcement investigators is the absolute right to counsel that attaches to the defendant when an accusatory instrument is filed. Since a defendant cannot waive his or her right to an attorney once this accusatory instrument is filed, is there any benefit to obtaining an arrest warrant? The answer is yes and no. If an arrest warrant exists, an accusatory instrument has been filed in court and any statement made to you by the defendant, even if he/she has waived Miranda rights, will be suppressed by the courts. This requirement is self-defeating for the investigator who wishes to complete the investigation by attempting to conduct an interrogation. If you are at the stage of your investigation where you are able to make an arrest and the whereabouts of the perpetrator are known to you, you may wish to consider making a warrantless arrest to protect your ability to interrogate the defendant if he/she chooses to waiver his/her Miranda rights.

Under most circumstances, arrests within a person's residence will require an arrest warrant. This requirement stems from the Fourth Amendment to the U.S. Constitution:

> The right of the people to be secure in their persons, houses, papers, and effects, against unreasonable searches and seizures, shall not be violated, and no Warrants shall issue, but upon probable cause, supported by Oath or affirmation, and particularly

* The People &c., Respondent, v. Corey Jones, Appellant. 2004 N.Y. Int. 46.

describing the place to be searched, and the persons or things to be seized.*

There are exceptions to this requirement, but again each state's laws will reflect its own historical experience in case law and legislation. One such universally accepted reason is the consent of the defendant to be arrested; another is to prevent the commission of a serious crime or to prevent the flight of the defendant who has committed or was in the process of committing a serious crime. There may be other exceptions under your state's laws, and you are advised to learn them and to discuss this issue with the prosecutor's office or your department's legal bureau.

There is no requirement under federal law to obtain a warrant of arrest. The Fourth Amendment only deals with a person's right to privacy within his or her own home or regular abode. If you observe a crime being committed, or you are informed by a reliable person that a crime has or is being committed, or if your investigation has revealed probable cause for the arrest, you can make the arrest without a warrant. Generally speaking, a warrantless arrest based on probable cause can take place anywhere except within the primary abode of the defendant, and even then there are exceptions as discussed earlier. Again, if you are at the prearrest stage, wish to attempt and interrogation, and know the whereabouts of the subject, you should attempt to make a warrantless arrest, either on the street, at the suspect's place of employment, or by staking out his residence or places that he is known to frequent, within the residence of a third party if it is not the regular abode of your subject, or, if the situation fits one of the exemptions, at his own residence. You are well advised to check with the prosecutor's office prior to a warrantless arrest at the subject's residence.

If you have exhausted all avenues of investigation but have not learned the whereabouts of a subject for whom you have probable cause for arrest, you may have no alternative but to seek an arrest warrant so that he/she can be apprehended nationally.

Another issue affecting the right to counsel may occur when the police are aware that the defendant is represented by an attorney on an unrelated criminal matter. Again, each state will address this in its own laws. But generally speaking if you are aware that the defendant is represented in an unrelated active criminal prosecution, you will not be able to question him or her regarding that unrelated matter, though you may still be able to interrogate regarding your current case.

The importance of knowing the federal and your state's legal requirements cannot be overstated. Remember, laws are dynamic rather than static.

* Bill of Rights, Fourth Amendment, U.S. Constitution.

Changing case law or decisions that are made by the courts relating to these matters will continue to impact your ability to conduct investigations. You must stay up to date with the legal requirements and maintain good relations with your local prosecutor's office.

5.3 Ready to Interrogate

Many techniques are being taught for the interrogation of suspects within the law enforcement community, such as the Reid Technique®, Practical Kinesic Interview & Interrogation ®, and Effective Interviewing and Interrogation Techniques by Nathan J. Gordon, among others. The author does not seek to endorse or criticize these or the other methods being advocated for use in interrogations; rather, we urge every professional investigator to fully research the art and science of interrogation in furtherance of his or her own skills.

In the military, interrogations are the responsibility of specialized intelligence units, and interrogation is a specialty assigned to highly trained members of the unit. In law enforcement there are no special units to conduct interrogations; rather, every investigator generally assumes the responsibility for interrogating his/her own defendants. It goes without saying that all interrogators are not created equally. Personality has a lot to do with a person's ability to conduct these special types of interviews. The U.S. Army indicates that "some desirable personal qualities in an interrogator are motivation, alertness, patience and tact, credibility, objectivity, self-control, adaptability, perseverance, and personal appearance and demeanor."[*] Additionally, a good interrogator needs to be a good actor, able to display different emotional postures as interrogations continue.

Obviously, not every investigator will possess these qualities; yet with study and practice they can be developed. Those investigators who do not possess or are unwilling to develop these abilities should allow interrogations to be conducted by those who do.

5.4 Know the Facts

If your interrogation is to be conducted with a defendant who was arrested at the scene, you will not have sufficient time to learn and analyze the history or the relationship between the victim and the defendant or the defendant's history; nor will you likely be able to learn more than the basic information from the crime scene. In essence, by interrogating a defendant at the scene,

[*] Headquarters, Dept. of the Army, Washington, DC, 8 May 1987: FM 34–52, Chap. 1.

you are trading off your base of knowledge for expediency, relying on the hope that the defendant will not have had the time to prepare defenses or excuses. These "strike while the iron is hot" interrogations can be very effective, especially in emotional situations where the victim and defendant are known to each other. Still, before beginning the interrogation, you should collect as much information as possible. First and foremost, you must find out if the defendant has been cooperative at the scene, if he/she has already been advised of Miranda, and if he/she has already made statements to the arresting officer or a third party. If the subject has been uncooperative at the scene, you should wait to conduct the interrogation at your office, where you will be in better control of the situation. If the defendant has been cooperative or has already confessed to a police officer or a third-party, you should advise him/her of his/her Miranda rights and attempt to record his/her confession at the scene. Remember, depending on your state's law or your department's guidelines, you may be required to videotape or audiotape the interrogation. The *Professional Investigators Series* recommends videotaping the entire interrogation process so as to eliminate claims of coercion, failure to advise of Miranda rights, or misrepresentation by police.

If the interrogation is to be conducted in a police or prosecutor's facility, a room with a two-way mirror serves several good purposes. In cases involving multiple defendants, it provides the opportunity for the intentionally "accidental" viewing of one defendant by the other during questioning without their hearing what is being said. This psychological ploy can be used to your advantage if you can play one defendant against the other. Another benefit may be derived from the defendant's belief that he/she is being observed but not whether it is by an eyewitness. A third benefit is that other investigators/interrogators can watch the behavior of the defendant and get a "feel" for his/her reactions and responses in the event that a change in interrogators becomes necessary.

Prior to beginning the interrogation, you should be completely familiar with all of the available information and facts regarding the crime scene, the victim and the defendant, their relationship, the motive, the witnesses, etc. You should formulate your questions ahead of time, but in a general rather than a specific order. Interrogations require flexibility rather than a rigid script. You will not know where the conversation will go until you begin.

Interrogations should be conducted by one investigator and certainly not more than two. If possible, the defendant should be unrestrained and the interrogators unarmed. It would be best if the room had no table so that nothing separates the defendant from the interrogator, leaving nothing for the defendant to hide behind, figuratively and psychologically. The interrogator(s) should position themselves between the defendant and the door, to reinforce the idea that the defendant is not free to leave. You have now set the stage for the interrogation by demonstrating that you are in charge. This is the mind set that both the interrogator and the defendant should be in for the duration of the session. If at any time you feel yourself losing control of the interrogation, you should stop and take the time necessary to compose yourself, or you may want to request that another interrogator take over.

You should reintroduce yourself to the defendant in a cordial but firm way, avoiding handshakes. Whether or not you are videotaping or recording the interrogation, a little small talk before reading the Miranda warnings can be beneficial in breaking the ice. You can ask the defendant if he or she needs anything, such as water, a snack, or a bathroom break, prior to beginning, yet you may wish to decline his/her unsolicited requests for a cigarettes, etc., again showing that you are in control. You should also use this small talk to gauge the intelligence and temperament of the defendant. If you believe that the defendant possesses below-average intelligence or is suffering from a mental illness, you should discontinue until you have had an opportunity to consult with the prosecutor.

5.5 Interrogating Juveniles

The Interrogation of a juvenile is yet another area where you may wish to consult with the prosecutor's office before continuing with an interrogation. The federal courts have indicated that parental consent is not necessary under Miranda, yet the youthfulness of defendants has been at the forefront of the discussion on false confessions. While federal law does not recognize the need for parental consent for Miranda warnings, each state has the ability to require additional safeguards for juveniles, such as the following.

> *per se* **age test:** The *per se* age test requires courts considering the voluntariness of juvenile confessions to rule that no confession given by a juvenile under a specified age (typically 14) can be admitted into evidence unless the youth is permitted, before or during the interrogation, to consult with a lawyer or other adult, preferably a family member, who is personally interested in the child's well-being. The adult acting on behalf of the juvenile must also be informed of the child's constitutional rights.[*]

---

[*] L. Szymanski, "Juvenile Waiver of *Miranda* Rights: Per Se Age Test," *NCJJ Snapshot* 7(3) (Pittsburgh, PA: National Center for Juvenile Justice, 2002).

5.6 Waiver of Miranda Rights by a Juvenile

Juveniles may waive their Miranda rights, and may do so without a parent being present. However, reviewing courts will closely review the facts and circumstances of the waiver to assure that it was voluntary. Many factors may be considered, including the juvenile's age, education, intelligence and emotional characteristics; his previous experience with the criminal justice system; the time of day and the presence of a parent or other adult concerned about the juvenile's welfare.

> In obtaining a Miranda waiver, great care should be taken to assure that the juvenile understands his/her rights. Mere recitation of the standard Miranda warnings will not be good enough. Law enforcement officers must take steps to ensure that the juvenile really understands his rights and the gravity of the situation. They must demonstrate that the juvenile has the mental capacity to comprehend the significance of *Miranda* and the rights waived. At minimum, officers should ask the juvenile to explain, in his own words, his understanding of each individual right. In certain cases (such as younger juveniles), officers might go so far as to explain what services an attorney might perform for the juvenile, and might take special care to explain the concept of self-incrimination.*

Remember, your mission is to obtain a true confession or to obtain information that will corroborate the guilt of the defendant. You do not want to obtain a false confession or one that will be suppressed by the court.

At this point you are ready to begin the interrogation, and even if the defendant has previously received Miranda warnings from yourself or others, you should now *read* them to the defendant again.

If the defendant consents to speaking with you after receiving the Miranda warnings, you should take a few minutes to ask pedigree and general questions regarding the defendant's education, lifestyle, relationships, etc., avoiding direct accusatory statements at this point. It is advantageous for you to have the defendant get used to answering your questions. It will also give you an opportunity to assess the defendant's style. Does he/she answer quickly and without hesitation? Are his/her answers long or short, to the point of rambling? It is important to look for changes in the defendant's style and demeanor as the interrogation proceeds.

---

* http://www.doj.state.wi.us/ss_manual/question.htm

Since this is a custodial interrogation, you are already in possession of enough evidence, be it physical, forensic, eyewitness, or circumstantial, to meet the "probable cause" requirement. In keeping with your responsibility to "control" the interview, you should begin by letting the defendant know that you already believe he/she committed the crime and that the purpose of the interview is to find out why. You have already done your homework and formulated general questions designed to move the interrogation toward the answers to specific facts. It is good to have these questions written on a steno pad so that you can read from it while turning the pages. You may want to refer back to this pad at certain times during the interrogation, usually after the defendant has finished answering a question truthfully, as if you are verifying what has been said. In this way, the defendant will begin to believe that you have a good command of the facts and that your steno book contains them.

As the interrogation continues, you may wish to confront the defendant with some of the facts you have learned, yet you should not reveal any facts that only the perpetrator of the crime would know. Rather, your goal is to get the defendant to tell you these facts without your suggesting them. Thus, you must avoid asking leading questions. Your questions must be clear, to the point, and open ended. The longer you can keep a defendant talking, the more information you will obtain, so long as the answer remains on topic. You must quickly and emphatically put a stop to rambling by the defendant and bring him or her back on track. Remember, keep control of the interrogation!

Some of the tools available to the interrogator and acknowledged by the courts are the ability to deceive, exaggerate, promise, warn of maximum criminal penalties, suggest how to obtain minimum sentences and pleas, religious beliefs, and guilty conscience. When using these techniques you must be careful not to become unbelievable in the eyes of the defendant. Once you lose your credibility with the defendant, you will have lost control over the interrogation. Be careful not to tell the defendant that you know something that is not possible. For example, if you know that the defendant has an older brother who lives with him, you might tell the defendant that you have spoken with his brother, who told you that the defendant bought a 9mm pistol last week. But it would be unfortunate for you if the brother was actually visiting his children in another state or was in a coma after an automobile accident. Know your facts before creating fictitious scenarios. Still, the proper creation of such fictions can be an invaluable tool. You may wish to tell the defendant that his fingerprints were found at the scene or on the weapon and then ask him to explain. You can let him know that the prosecutor will consider lesser charges if he (the defendant) is truthful with you. You can tell the defendant that one or more eyewitnesses have identified him. You can empathize with the defendant by telling him that you would have done the same thing under the same circumstances, for example, if you caught your wife cheating. You can use the time-tested "good cop/bad cop" scenario, where the good cop comes to the defense of the defendant while the bad cop is in the accusatory mode. You can use one, all, or any of these or additional ruses and ploys during the interrogation. The key is your ability to be flexible and to recognize the current and changing states of mind of the defendant.

Again, from an investigative standpoint the best confession obtainable will be the one in which the defendant reveals information linking him to the crime that has not been disclosed to him by you or anyone else and that only the perpetrator would have knowledge of. These pieces of information should be closely guarded, yet your questioning must be designed to lead the defendant to these facts.

If you have videotaped or at least audiotaped the entire interrogation, it will not be necessary to reduce the defendant's confession to writing. If you have not recorded the entire interrogation, you should now memorialize the confession, either in writing or by videotape or audiotape. This memorialization should include either a written or a verbal waiver of the Miranda warnings, the date, the time, the place, the case name/number, and the identity of everyone present.

5.7 Closing Cases with No Arrest

It is a fairly common perception within the professional law enforcement community that most murders are solved within a few days. In large part this is due to the fact that persons known to the victim commit the majority of murders. Thorough and competent investigations will result in the arrest of a certain additional number of unfamiliar-victim/-perpetrator cases as well.

If after your best efforts your case still remains a mystery, all is not lost. Most states have no statute of limitations on murder. There is no set time limit for keeping your investigation active. But if you are in a location with an active caseload and after a month you have not uncovered any new information to move the case along, you may want to deactivate it pending new information. Prior to doing so, you should conduct a complete review of the case and chronologically document everything that was done, any items that remain outstanding, and your theories. You will then be able to conduct periodic reviews, check for similar cases, touch base with informants, etc. A well-documented case will also allow other investigators who follow you to pick up where you left off. Many homicides have been solved years after the fact.

Robbery Investigations

6

Robbery is one of the four violent crimes categorized by the FBI's uniform crime reports, the others being murder, forcible rape, and aggravated assault. This book is constructed in such a way as to cover the most difficult aspects of criminal investigation first, starting with the crime scene and death investigations. By utilizing the same techniques that have been previously discussed, the investigator already possesses two thirds of the knowledge required to investigate the crime of robbery. This section relates to robbery as a stand-alone crime, rather than a crime committed in conjunction with a murder or a rape.

A good working definition of a robbery is the taking of someone else's property by force or intimidation (threat of force). As a stand-alone crime, robbery, unlike murder, forcible rape, or aggravated assault, usually has only one motive, greed. The force or threat of force necessary for a robbery to occur can best be described as *any*, with lesser criminal penalties for the use of minimal physical force, a greater degree of penalty for force that causes injury or for robberies in which accomplices are present, and maximum criminal penalty for serious physical injuries during robberies committed with the use of deadly and/or dangerous weapons. While the legal definition of robbery and the various degrees of the crime may vary from state to state, this basic concept remains the same.

Police detectives will rarely investigate physical-force robberies that do not involve an injury or a theft of significant value. That is not to say that all purse snatches, stolen jackets, school lunch money crimes, etc., are ignored; rather, most police departments cannot provide the investigative manpower necessary to investigate every crime and therefore they prioritize their workload. Additionally, many physical force-/intimidation-only robberies involve persons who are known to each other from school, family, or neighborhoods, and often an arrest or the initial investigation is conducted by uniformed officers. Purse and chain snatch robberies will usually present a "pattern," such as street location, time of day, nature of victim, or use of vehicle, that should be detected at the local level by the officers charged with the responsibility of analyzing crime. The use of patrol or plainclothes anti-crime or crime prevention officers would be better suited to the apprehension of these types of criminals.

When dealing with random, opportunistic types of armed robberies this same use of patrol officers and plainclothes officers can be of great value when working with detectives. By this means, stakeouts, stings, and decoy operations can be coordinated and executed. These types of robberies are usually committed within the same general area in which the perpetrator resides and/or "fits in." There is generally little or no planning other than the element of surprise of the victim. The review and analysis of all armed robbery cases by detectives is necessary to identify when, where, who, and how these crimes are being committed.

Organized armed robberies require planning and execution on the part of the robber or the robbery team. A well-orchestrated robbery is the result of foreknowledge acquired by the perpetrator(s) during exploratory visits, or "casings," of the potential site of the robbery or by obtaining "inside" information from a willing or unwitting accomplice. This type of robbery investigation must start with the premise that the robbers have done this before. The intelligence and analysis operation is of little value in death investigations other than those involving serial killers, but it is invaluable in the investigation of robbery and burglary cases. In the past this intelligence-gathering operation was a difficult undertaking, usually involving manual review of reports and the recording of information to written files or index card systems. Today, computers with relational databases have the ability to compile great amounts of useful information on crimes being committed within a precinct, a city, a state, and the entire nation.

Whether it's a random or a well-planned robbery, the investigator must examine the methods, words used, weapons used, actions of all participants, and potential disposition of the acquired property that has been stolen. Robbery is generally not a one-time crime; rather, robbers will continue to commit similar crimes using similar methods.

The investigation of armed robbery requires that the crime scene be safe-guarded and processed for the collection of evidence, that witnesses be segregated and interviewed, and that a canvass be conducted. In that way this type of investigation is similar to a death investigation, yet there are several significant differences: (1) a live victim, (2) known entrance/actions/exit of perpetrator(s), (3) motive, (4) potential pattern—*modus operandi*, (5) known proceeds of crime (money, jewelry, art, etc.) (6) known weapon (either general or specific), (7) use of intelligence and analysis, (8) use of informants.

6.1 Robbery Victims

Victims of armed robberies are usually surprised, confused, and unnerved. Three conditions that can and often do contribute to inaccurate recollection of facts. Additionally, crime victims may be fearful of the judicial system itself, either because of past personal experience, fear of reprisal if they prosecute, or fear of future loss of time or income.

Being a victim means ceding control of your life to the criminal. It may take several minutes, hours, days, or sometimes years before the victim can recover from this loss of control. The victim may also blame the police for a failure to protect them or for the length of time it took for police officers to respond to the victim's call for help. Investigators must keep these possibilities in mind when meeting with and interviewing victims, and they must act accordingly by being empathetic, consoling, supportive, and confidently reassuring.

If the victim is emotional or agitated at the scene, the initial interview should be limited to the information required to substantiate that a crime has been committed: obtaining the identity or description of the perpetrators, the perpetrators' actions at the scene, including areas that may contain latent fingerprints, the property taken, and the mode and direction of flight. This information should be used to broadcast an alarm. If the victim requires medical assistance, he/she should be transported to an emergency room by ambulance, accompanied by a police officer. If no medical treatment is required, the victim should then be transported to the detective's office, where he/she should be made comfortable, provided with food and/or beverage, and placed in a relaxed atmosphere. The victim should not be placed in a position where he or she can observe prisoners, suspects, interrogations, or the turmoil usually associated with police facilities.

The interview should be conducted in as pleasant a surrounding as possible, avoiding windowless two-way mirrored interrogation rooms. The victim should not be placed in a corner or in a position where you are between him/her and the exit. Remember, the victim has already lost control over his/her actions once that day, and you should avoid making him/her feel that way again. On the contrary, you should do anything within reason to empower the victim, such as encouraging him/her to ask for food, make contact with friends or relatives, or anything else requested that you can accomplish. By having someone do as he or she asks, the victim will begin to regain confidence and control. Additionally, you are about to have the individual recall a traumatic event, one that he/she may rather consciously or subconsciously forget. It is advantageous for the investigator to build a rapport with the victim and to put him/her at ease.

Once the interview begins, you should take the time to reintroduce yourself and to assure the victim that everything possible will be done to help and to recover their property. Do not take any hostility toward you personally; rather, if it surfaces, you should try to redirect this emotion toward the robber. You can let the victim know that you truly understand what he/she is feeling, not just as a professional investigator but also as a person. You may wish to tell the victim that you or a family member has been victimized in the same way and that you understand what he or she is feeling. It is important to gain the victim's trust and to let that person know you are concerned about what has happened.

Flexibility is the basis for any interview. You as the investigator should have a thorough knowledge of the crime and the crime scene before conducting an in-depth interview of the victim. You should not have a prepared script or read to the victim from a prepared list of questions, yet you should have a general idea of the questions that need to be answered. The last thing you would want to do is limit the victim to short or yes/no answers. Avoid letting the victim start the narrative at the point of the robbery; rather, have the person begin with an earlier part of the day and work forward. In this manner you will get him/her into the habit of relating information to you, beginning with less stressful occurrences and leading up to and through the robbery.

You should allow talkative victims to tell their own story at their own pace and encourage nontalkative victims to help you help them. During the victim's recital you should listen for the obvious who, what, why, where, when, and how and take note of which issues need further exploration. You will have the opportunity to compare the victim's recollection to the information you have learned from the crime scene, other witnesses, and other police officers and investigators.

There may be times during this interview when the victim falters or hesitates, but these pauses should not be allowed to go on for too long. Eye contact and a simple nod may be all it takes to get the victim talking again, or short, positive acknowledgments, such as "That's great! What happened next?" or a smile followed by "Go ahead" may get them talking again. While the victim is talking you should avoid asking questions; allow the victim to tell his/her story uninterrupted. This is not to say that you should allow the victim to go off on tangents unrelated to the incident or avoid speaking about the robbery itself; rather, you should gently guide the victim back on track. You should avoid taking detailed notes at this point; rather, you should listen attentively to what the victim has to say, making mental notes and if necessary jotting down any significant items quickly without interrupting the flow of interview.

Once you have heard the victim's story in its entirety you will be able to review the events with him/her as you have heard them, allowing the victim the opportunity to verify, correct, or add to the information. During your review you may want to make one or two intentional minor mistakes to ensure that the victim is paying attention and to refocus him/her on the events. This is the point at which you should take detailed notes and ask the questions that remain unanswered. The questions that you do ask should be open ended rather than leading. It is much better to ask, "Did the robber have an accent?" than "Did the robber have a Spanish accent?"

Once you have fully reviewed the interview with the victim, a formal statement should be taken, in either written, audiotape, or videotape format. A proper heading or introduction should be placed on the record, including the date, time, place, identity of the victim and of all persons present, the case or complaint number, and the nature of the crime. If the victim does not consent to this statement, do not force the issue. Use your handwritten notes to prepare your formal investigation report, and preserve your notes in the file in the event of a trial.

Many different interview techniques are being advocated for witness interviews or interrogations. It is entirely up to you whether to choose a static/dynamic approach that focuses on one specific occurrence (static) or on a series of occurrences (dynamic), or the cognitive approach developed by Professors Ronald P. Fisher of Florida International University and Edward Geiselman of UCLA, which has the witness recall the day of the event in different sequences and from different perspectives, or the Reid technique, or behavioral observation, or linguistic analysis, etc., It would be beneficial for every investigator to explore these and other interview techniques and develop an expertise in the art of interviewing. Whether you choose to use any of these interview techniques or one of your own, it is essential to create an atmosphere of trust, rapport, and confidence with the witness prior to and during the interview. If the victim feels you are disinterested, disorganized, or disingenuous, he/she will be less likely to recall facts or be cooperative.

Finally, there is no such thing as a standard interview or an allotted amount of time to give to a victim or for that matter any witness. You should expect to spend as much time as the victim is willing to give, but you should not demand more than that. It is your job to make unwilling witnesses cooperative and to keep cooperative ones on the right track. Remember, if you are successful in your investigation, your victim will become a plaintiff in a criminal action. If you have alienated the victim during the initial or subsequent interviews or if you have lied to or misled them regarding their part in the criminal justice system, you will have created a negative impact on any future prosecutions.

Once the interview is over, you will now know if the victim can identify the robber(s) by viewing photographs, assist in developing a composite sketch, identify tattoos, scars, birthmarks, accents, speech patterns, or any other identifying attributes. If the victim can, you should encourage the victim to visit the identification unit immediately, while the incident is fresh in mind, rather than returning on another day. If no positive identification is made, let the victim know that these investigations are ongoing and that you may contact him/her to view photographs or lineups in the future. If the witness cannot provide any assistance in identifying the perpetrator(s), you should thank him/her for cooperating and explain what he/she can expect as your investigation continues, up to and through a prosecution.

6.2 Eyewitness Interviews

Aside from the victim, there may have been additional eyewitnesses to the robbery. As with witnesses at death scenes, it is always best to segregate and interview eyewitnesses alone. Multiple witnesses will not always provide information or descriptions that are consistent with one another's. You should expect minor differences in descriptions of perpetrators, and events. Substantial differences should be a cause for concern, and every effort should be made to clarify these issues as quickly as possible. People will focus on different things, depending on their observation point, fear factor, life experiences, and other outside influences. A barber may pay particular attention to hairstyle and color, while a fashion designer may recall clothing, etc. Someone looking down the barrel of a sawed-off shotgun may not be able to tell you if the person holding the gun had brown or blue eyes or was six feet tall or five feet tall, even though that person may have been standing three feet away. The focus will likely be on the gun. On the other hand, someone standing 30 feet to the side may be able to provide an accurate identification of the perpetrators, including their clothing. Again, the investigator conducting these interviews should attempt to establish a rapport with the witnesses, guide them to begin their story at some point before the actual incident so that they become comfortable relating information to the detective and to allow or encourage them to tell their whole story without interruption. Their story can then be repeated to them by the detective, followed by nonleading questions for clarification.

When dealing with eyewitnesses to crimes, the investigator needs to keep in mind issues of distance, lighting, obstructions, vision or hearing problems, age, physiological and mental conditions, or any other matters that may affect the observations. After the initial interviews, investigators should conduct thorough background investigations of all witnesses, to include whether or not they have ever provided eyewitness testimony before. If a positive identification has been made, any relationship between the witness and the suspect should be explored.

6.3 Eyewitness Identifications

In recent years the credibility of eyewitness identifications of strangers has been called into question. Advances in DNA identification have freed numerous persons who had been wrongfully convicted at trials, in part because of faulty or intentionally false eyewitness identifications. Many claims have been made, some indicating that 50% or more of eyewitness identifications are false. The validity of eyewitness identification of persons known to them, no matter how remote the relationship, has not been disputed.

Psychologists such as Gary L. Wells, professor of psychology at Iowa State University, have conducted numerous studies on memory as it relates to eyewitness recollections in criminal matters and concluded that eyewitnesses are generally unreliable. As reported in the April 7, 2003, edition of the *Washington Post*, Dr. Wells and his researchers

> prepared a 60-second videotape purportedly showing a man on a roof dropping what appears to be a bomb down an air shaft. They showed the tape to 253 volunteers, who were then asked to pick out the bomber from six photographs. Unknown to the volunteer witnesses, a picture of the actor playing the bomber was not in the array. Nevertheless, every volunteer picked a suspect. After making their choice, some were told they made the right choice, some told they made the wrong one, and some were told nothing. They were then asked how well they remembered what they saw in the video. The people who were told they picked the right suspect had much greater confidence in virtually all aspects of their recollection, and 23% said they were at least 90% sure of details. Those given no feedback were much less confident, with only 2% saying they were at least 90% sure. The researchers said the findings affirm the recommendation that police lineups be "double-blind," with neither the witness nor the investigator accompanying the witness told whether the right suspect was chosen.[*]

[*] David Brown, *Washington Post*, April 7, 2003, p. A07.

6.4 Arrests Based on Witness Identification

Studies such as these are placing new pressures on the criminal justice system with respect to eyewitness identifications, yet there have been few if any changes in the investigative process. There are generally four ways for arrests to be made based on eyewitness identification: (1) at the scene of the crime, (2) a show-up or one-on-one identification within a short time of the commission of the crime, (3) photo array, preferably followed by (4) a physical lineup. A fifth way occurs when the witness sees the defendant at a later time and notifies the police. Arrests made at the scene are rarely challenged as misidentifications, and these cases rarely go to a trial.

A "show-up" usually occurs when a suspect is apprehended shortly after the crime, usually within 2–3 hours, and either brought back to the scene for an identification, or when the victim or witnesses are summoned to the police station for a one-on-one viewing. Show-ups are best used in cases where the victim had a substantial amount of face-to-face time with the suspect (several minutes), with adequate lighting and no obstructions at the scene, and when the victim was able to provide an accurate description of the suspect prior to the apprehension.

A photo-array can be shown to witnesses after a suspect has been determined. A group of similar photographs that depict similar persons should be constructed. Similar photographs are those taken by the same type of camera with the same type of film and a similar background. A Polaroid photo of the suspect placed in an array with five 35mm photographs would certainly make it stick out, as would a color photo of the suspect when placed with five black-and-white photos. In the same way, suspects should be shown with persons of the same race, sex, and general features, such as mustaches, eyeglasses, and haircuts. One problem with this type of showing has been addressed by Dr. Wells and others: The witness may believe that one of the photographs being shown to them must be of the perpetrator, and the witness will feel an obligation to make an identification. It has been suggested that witnesses be told that a suspect's photograph may or may not be in the array, yet this is unlikely to convince a witness that the police would waste time by showing them photographs of nonsuspects only. If a positive identification is made based on a photo-array, it is recommended that a physical lineup be conducted. Yet, according to Dr. Wells' studies, a person who has been told that he/she correctly identified the perpetrator will become more confident and that at a subsequent physical lineup the witness will be making an identification based on the photo rather than their actual memory.

Physical lineups are generally conducted using two-way mirrors. Again, the suspect should be placed with at least five other persons of the same race, approximate age, height, weight, hair, glasses, mustaches, clothing, etc. Lineups can be done standing or sitting. Each person in the lineup should be treated in the same fashion. If one is asked to stand up or turn around or speak certain words, they should all be asked to do the same thing. Every precaution must be taken to avoid conscious or subconscious hints. Again, challenges to eyewitness identifications at lineups are based on witness perceptions that the criminal must be in the lineup, since the police would not waste everyone's time by conducting a lineup of innocent people only.

In eyewitness identification–only cases, it is the responsibility of the investigator to thoroughly document any alibis provided by the suspect. Or if the suspect has exercised his/her rights under Miranda, you as the investigator should make all reasonable efforts to determine the suspect's whereabouts at the time of the robbery, including speaking to relatives, neighbors, coworkers, employers, etc.

In cases where physical evidence such as DNA or fingerprints implicates a suspect, an eyewitness's identification can be viewed as icing on the cake. The same holds true where a defendant has confessed to the crime. Yet where eyewitness identification is the only evidence linking a defendant to a crime, the investigator is often left with little or no choice but to make an arrest. The police investigator's obligation is to effect arrests based on probable cause, in other words, on information that would lead a reasonable person to believe the suspect committed the crime. Without evidence to the contrary, a victim's or an eyewitness, positive identification must serve as that level of probable cause. You cannot tell a victim that an arrest cannot be made because of the studies conducted by Dr. Wells and others. The concept of "guilty beyond a reasonable doubt" belongs to the trial court, not law enforcement.

6.5 *Modus Operandi*

Crime analysis and the intelligence-gathering function cannot be underestimated in the investigation of robberies. While investigations of serial killers and serial rapists get high-profile exposure in the media, these crimes occur at a far lesser rate than armed robbery and are generated by a deep-seated psychological impairment. When examining serial murders and rapists, investigators will attempt to construct a profile by looking for psychological anomalies such as domination, disfigurements, disemboweling, fetishes, or other signature issues. These signature issues do not generally come into play in armed robberies, where the primary motivation is monetary.

Most every mid-size to large police department will have a specialized unit to deal with armed robbery or the analysis of violent crimes. By analyzing the actions and words of the perpetrators, these units will attempt to discover if the same perpetrator is committing multiple robberies. The methods used, or the MO, can be very revealing and can include such things as (1) type of robbery, e.g., from a person, a business, a bank, etc., (2) type of weapon used, (3) time of day, day of week, etc., (4) specific words spoken, accents, speech patterns, etc., (5) attire, mask, disguise, (6) actions at scene, e.g., jumping over counters, demanding money or reaching into registers, making victims lay face down, locking victims in rooms, (7) knowledge of crime scene or evidence of prior casing, (8) getaways and warnings to victims, or any other method that displays itself in multiple cases.

As you look for similarities in crimes, you must keep an open mind and realize that professional criminals can learn from their mistakes. MOs should be viewed as dynamic, with the potential to change as time goes by.

If you are an investigator in a smaller department that does not have a specialized robbery or crime analysis section, you should take this responsibility on yourself. This information will aid you in many ways; e.g., you may be able to plan "stakeouts," have witnesses from the various crimes view photo-arrays or lineups, share information with other units or departments, or utilize the information during interrogations or victim/witness interviews in subsequent cases, etc.

6.6 Informants and Robbery Investigations

In the world of politics, a popular saying is "All politics is local." To a great extent this theory holds true for the commission of crimes as well. Most criminals operate within their own geographic area, though not necessarily within their own immediate community. As an investigator it is important to develop contacts and sources of information within your geographical area of employment. These sources can include local businesspeople, media contacts, bartenders, concerned citizens, criminals, and people motivated by revenge, financial gain. Of these groups, the criminals may be the most productive when seeking information about the identities of perpetrators of armed robberies or other crimes.

To a large extent, how informants are handled depends on the policies and procedures of your department or agency. More than likely, there will be some sort of confidential registration procedure that will include a background check, the reason for cooperation, e.g., monetary, reduced criminal sentencing, community concerns, etc., and a periodic review of their performance. You may also develop more casual sources of information as your tenure within the community increases, including those who do not wish to become registered as informants. The use of unregistered informants may be useful, so long as they are willing to come forward and cooperate within the judicial system or you are able to independently verify their information through other investigative means. One problem with unregistered informants will be their lack of historical reliability, or a "track record."

Whether or not your information comes from a registered informant, your actions must comply with the federal and state laws governing your area. The most comprehensive guidelines for the registration and management of confidential informants is provided by the U.S. Department of Justice, titled *The Attorney General's Guidelines Regarding the Use of Confidential Informants.*[*] The reading of these guidelines is strongly recommended.

In criminal investigations, the primary use of confidential informants is in the area of narcotics enforcement (see Chapter 8, "Narcotics Investigations"). Since the vast majority of informants will be registered to narcotics detectives, you should seek to develop good working relationships with those investigators. The sharing of information is a two-way street, and for the narcotics investigator you can be a source of introduction to new potential informants. With this in mind, and to the extent possible during interviews and interrogations, you should explore the person's knowledge of criminal activity, specific crimes, and perpetrators and assess the person's potential as a confidential informant.

[*] http://www.usdoj.gov/olp/dojguidelines.pdf

Burglary Investigations

7

Burglary can be classified into one of two distinct categories: (1) residential or (2) commercial. As with other crimes, each state will have its own definition and criminal penalties. Yet whether the crime is called "burglary," "breaking and entering," or something else, the elements of the crime will be the same. A burglary occurs when a person illegally enters a premise with the intent to commit a crime inside.

7.1 Residential Burglary

The most common burglaries are those committed where people live. In general, a burglar operates by stealth and seeks to avoid observation or confrontation. Occasionally a burglary will escalate into a more violent crime, such as robbery, assault, rape, or homicide, but this generally occurs only if the burglar is interrupted during the commission of the crime.

While burglary is considered to be a property crime, it does have a direct psychological impact on the victims whose home has been intruded upon. The victims will feel a loss of control over their personal environment, security, peace of mind, and well-being.

In most highly populated areas, police departments will set a minimum dollar threshold on the investigation of burglaries by detectives. Some departments may have specially trained uniformed officers to respond to residential burglaries to take the reports and process the crime scene for fingerprints and other forensic evidence, such as tool marks. The results of these mini-crime-scene investigations can be very useful in crime analysis and in linking perpetrators to other crimes through latent prints or other physical evidence. Larger departments may have "specialty" units with the responsibility for investigating the crimes of burglary and larceny, otherwise referred to as *property crimes.*

In cases where the population density is less severe or when the stolen property meets or exceeds the department's monetary threshold, a detective is usually assigned. As a property crime, burglary will not receive the same amount of attention from the uniformed force as a death scene or a robbery. In all likelihood, no uniformed supervisor will be present, and less attention will be paid to the crime scene. Furthermore, as the detective assigned to this case you may not receive notification of the crime until the police officer that responded drops off the report. While this delay is certainly responsible for the loss of physical evidence, the crime scene must still be processed in accordance with the accepted principals of investigation. It is through fingerprints, DNA, trace evidence, tool marks, canvassing for witnesses, etc., that many burglary investigations are solved.

Starting with the obvious point of entry, you should walk through the crime scene with the victim to determine the areas within the residence that were disturbed by the burglar. If there is no obvious point of entry or exit, you should pay particular attention to the doors and windows for evidence of tampering and tool marks. More than likely, the victim has had time to inventory his/her valuable possessions and will be able to show you where the stolen property was taken from. These areas may include closets, drawers, refrigerators, home safes, display cabinets, etc. Try to reconstruct the burglar's activities and movements while inside the residence, and keep your eyes open for anything that may have been dropped by the burglar along the way, such as a wallet, ID cards, pictures, or laundry tickets. Ask the victim if he/she has found anything at the scene that does not belong to him/her. As at any other crime scene, you will also be looking for fingerprints, impressions, transfer evidence, blood and other bodily materials, fibers, etc.

The proper and thorough identification of the stolen property is also essential to the investigation. In addition to currency, burglars will remove jewelry, electronics, art, collectables, and other items of value they can resell, pawn, or otherwise market. As the investigator, you should obtain serial numbers, photographs, descriptions, or other means of positively identifying the stolen property.

A canvass of neighbors should be conducted as soon as possible, paying special attention to issues of strangers and suspicious vehicles that may have been observed in the area prior to the burglary.

The majority of arrests for burglary are made by uniformed officers at or near the scene during their response to a "burglary in progress" call. The identity and subsequent interview of the 911 callers is essential to the prosecution or, if no arrest has been made, to the investigation of the crime. An interrogation should be attempted of all persons arrested for burglary for the purpose of recovering property, solving other crimes, and cultivating possible confidential informants.

With the exception of currency, most burglars have little or no consistent means of converting property into cash other than through a "fence," a person who specializes in purchasing stolen property. This "fence" can be a local business, such as a pawnshop, an appliance or electronics dealer, or a jeweler, or another criminal, etc., with the ability to move the property back into the stream of commerce. The goal of the burglary investigator should be to follow the trail of property to the end user, thereby identifying and arresting all persons who have illegally received or transferred it. The use of a confidential informant can be invaluable in introducing an undercover police officer into the criminal enterprise.

Another investigative tool that can be used is the "sting operation." Simply stated, a sting operation is an orchestrated role-playing, covert police operation within which undercover officers pose as "fences" and purchase stolen merchandise from criminals. These operations can be set up as local businesses, e.g., bars, grocery stores, used tire stores, or they can operate out of an apartment or home. The intent is for word to spread throughout the criminal community so that a regular clientele of burglars can be developed. The merchandise that is purchased can be traced back to particular crimes, eventually being returned to the proper owners. The identities of the burglars are confirmed during these operations, and some if not all of them may be placed under surveillance so that they can be caught in the act. At the end of the operation is a mass arrest of all the people that have sold the stolen merchandise to the undercover officers. Through the use of sting operations, many other crimes are solved as well. It is important to attempt interrogations of all those who have been arrested for their knowledge of other criminal enterprises, robberies, murders, etc.

7.2 Commercial Burglary

Commercial burglaries, that is, those committed against businesses, fall into two basic categories: planned and unplanned. The unplanned burglaries are usually desperate, "smash and grab" crimes committed by one or two low-level street criminals. Jewelry and electronics retailers are favorite targets for this type of crime, because the stolen property can usually be transported easily and sold quickly.

Planned burglaries are more likely to be committed by professional thieves acting as a group. Most planned commercial burglaries occur over weekends, holidays, and extended holiday weekends, when many commercial establishments are closed. Organized gangs will usually target facilities located away from residential areas so that the potential number of witnesses will be limited or nonexistent. Warehouses, large retail and manufacturing facilities, banks, etc., are prime targets since they will usually have money and valuable products that are easily disposed of.

The planning for such crimes can include surveillance of the location by the crime group prior to the burglary, inside information obtained by coercion of an existing employee, or having one of the gang obtain employment at the company.

It is not uncommon for these types of gangs to use sophisticated electronic and power equipment to defeat alarm systems, dig tunnels, or make holes in walls or roofs. The damage caused to the physical plants themselves is usually far greater in commercial burglaries than in residential ones.

7.3 Crime Analysis/Commercial Burglary

Professional burglary groups will usually present themselves in a pattern of crimes that may be regional in nature. Crime analysis and multijurisdictional cooperation is essential for the successful investigation of these organized gangs.

7.4 Crime Scene/Commercial Burglary

As with any other major crime investigation, good crime scene procedures must be followed to document the scene and to identify and collect evidence. The criminals' ingress and egress may be easily discovered, e.g., obvious break-ins, or they may be impossible to discover, as in entering with a legitimate key. In either case, a complete and thorough search for tools, tool marks, and "pick marks" on locks will need to be conducted and documented. Most successful burglary gangs will repeat their successful efforts and provide clues through their MO or by a specific type of signature, such as leaving writings on walls or floors or scratch marks. This type of information is invaluable to crime analysts.

Once the crime scene is processed, an inventory of all items stolen should be obtained, including all serial and model numbers of equipment and detailed description of jewelry, etc.

7.5 Canvass/Commercial Burglary

In addition to seeking witnesses to the actual crime, the commercial burglary canvass should focus on any suspicious activities that occurred in the area in the weeks leading up to the crime. A check of all police responses to calls in the area should be made, as well as a review of all traffic and parking violations issued.

7.6 Insurance Frauds and Inside Jobs

In cases where no physical evidence of a break-in exists, the possibility of an inside job must be considered. Even in cases where there is an obvious break-in, the investigator must keep in mind the possibility of an inside job or an insurance fraud through a falsely reported staged burglary.

If a fraudulent claim is suspected, investigators should feel free to request bills of lading and all invoices and records relating to the purchase and receipt by the company of merchandise that is being reported as stolen. Investigators can also request copies of all records relating to the normal deliveries made by the business during the past month, as well as the daily vehicle logs from the company's delivery trucks to see where deliveries were made and the mileage that was recorded. Any inconsistencies with respect to usual mileage, the number of deliveries made to regular customers, or the trucks being dispatched with unusually light loads should be viewed as suspicious. During interviews of owners and employees, questions regarding the financial health of the business should be asked.

If the investigator suspects that the criminals had inside information in the commission of the burglary (e.g., no signs of forced entry, knowledge of hidden safes), the investigator may wish to speak with the owner or personal manager regarding any recently dismissed or disgruntled employees, recent hires, employees with financial problems, employees found wandering or loitering in areas of the business where they should not be, etc. Criminal-record searches should be conducted on all employees, if practical, or on only those suspected of possible involvement if there are too many employees at the location.

7.7 Follow-Up Investigation in Commercial Burglary

As in residential burglaries, the organized gang will need the means to convert the property into cash. Since most burglaries of this nature require extensive planning, it is logical to assume that the gang had previously arranged for the disposal of the merchandise. Investigators may wish to visit retail and wholesale outlets within their jurisdiction and request other agencies in the region to make these visits in an effort to identify any of the stolen merchandise. Investigators may also notify the manufacturer of the products and ask them to "red flag" any warranty work on products with the stolen serial numbers.

It is also possible that the burglary gang is using a professional "fence" to dispose of the merchandise.

If heavy equipment or power tools were used during the commission of the commercial burglary, investigators should contact equipment rental businesses in the area to determine who may have rented such equipment. If such equipment is actually located, the investigator may choose to have the equipment processed by crime scene technicians for any evidence that could tie it to the crime scene, e.g., dirt, paint, cement, metal filings, fingerprints, DNA.

It may also be advantageous for the investigator to check on recent commercial rentals in the area that may have been used by the gang during their planning or to store the stolen property.

Finally, the use of informants and sting operations can also be effective in the investigation of commercial burglaries.

Narcotics Investigations

8

The "war on drugs" became a popular expression in 1972, when it was first used by President Richard Nixon to describe the nation's drug enforcement programs. But despite the hundreds of billions of dollars, immeasurable investigative man-hours, arrests, trials, and incarcerations, the problems associated with the sale and use of illegal drugs continue. The cost to our society from the cultivation, processing, importation, distribution, and use of these illicit substances cannot be measured in dollars; rather, it must be considered in terms of human misery, health care costs, lost productivity, and the escalation in violent and property crimes. While this war is still waging, the prospects for total victory appear to be dim. Yet as a society we have taken the positions that illegal drugs must be eliminated and that drug dealers and at times drug users must be detected, prosecuted, and jailed. To this end, specialized narcotics investigation units have been developed at the federal, state, and local levels.

According to the U.S. Department of Justice, Bureau of Justice Statistics: "In 2003 the Federal Bureau of Investigation's Uniform Crime Reports (UCR) estimated that there were 1,678,192 state and local arrests for drug abuse violations in the United States.[*]

At the federal level, since 1973 the Drug Enforcement Administration (DEA) has evolved as the primary investigative unit, with the FBI having concurrent jurisdiction over drug offenses under the Controlled Substances Act.

Part of the DEA's mission is to work with foreign governments to detect and eradicate the cultivation of crops, the processing labs, and the shipping systems. Domestically, the DEA works with other federal agencies, such as

---

[*] FBI, *Uniform Crime Reports*, Crime in the United States, annually.

91

Customs, Border Patrol, Treasury, the Internal Revenue Service, and the military and with state and local agencies to enforce the laws that cover "controlled substances." (See the next section.) There are currently over 4,000 investigators employed by the DEA.

At the state and local levels, narcotics enforcement is a primary responsibility of most state, city, and county police departments and sheriffs' offices. In addition, many district attorney's or prosecutor's offices will have specialized narcotics units. The vast majority of these law enforcement agencies participate in multijurisdictional task forces that foster cooperation and coordination across jurisdictional boundaries and governmental levels.

> In 2000, about 9 in 10 local police departments regularly performed drug enforcement functions. More than 90% of the departments in each population category of 2,500 or more had drug enforcement responsibilities, including all of those serving 100,000 or more residents. Departments with drug enforcement responsibilities employed 98% of all local police officers[*]

> In 2000, 95% of sheriffs' offices regularly performed drug enforcement functions.[†]

Investigative techniques, tools, and laws have also evolved over time and now include the conversion of illegally gained currency, vehicles, planes, marine vessels, homes, and other assets commonly referred to as "asset forfeiture." Depending on the jurisdiction, these proceeds of the illegal drug trade may be converted to state or local treasuries, kept by law enforcement agencies for use in continued operations, or sold at auction, with the proceeds being distributed in accordance with the law.

8.1 The Controlled Substances Act (CSA)

Title II of the Comprehensive Drug Abuse Prevention and Control Act of 1970 classifies drugs into five "schedules" of drugs, with schedule 1 being the most harmful or addictive, with little or no recognized medical value, and schedule 5 being the least harmful. The CSA is flexible, so drugs can be added, deleted, or moved from one schedule to another. The schedules can be reviewed at http://www.usdoj.gov/dea/pubs/csa/812.htm.

---

[*] Bureau of Criminal Justice Statistics, *Local Police Departments 2000*, NCJ 196002, January 2003.
[†] Bureau of Criminal Justice Statistics, *Sheriffs' Offices 2000*, NCJ 196534, January 2003.

As demonstrated by these schedules, not all controlled substances are derived from the cultivation of foreign crops, nor are they all illegally manufactured overseas. Many of these drugs are manufactured at clandestine laboratories within the United States. Additionally, the diversion of legally manufactured pharmaceuticals for sale by illicit-drug dealers is of equal concern to law enforcement. This diversion of otherwise legal prescription drugs can take place at many points within the stream of commerce, e.g., manufacturing, shipping, retail pharmacies, hospitals, doctors' offices, and forgery of prescriptions.

8.2 Organized Crime

The sale of illegal drugs is a highly profitable enterprise that involves sophisticated distribution networks to move the product from fields and laboratories located around the world to the end user. There are many separate organized criminal networks from countries around the world that operate independent of one another, sometimes in conjunction with each other, not only to distribute their products, but to launder the profits as well. Unlike violent or property crimes, narcotics distribution is an ongoing enterprise that operates 24 hours a day, 365 days a year. The investigation of this crime requires different tools and methods at various stages and geographic locations, be it internationally, nationally, regionally, or locally. More so than any other type of investigation, drug cases require coordination through an ongoing team concept.

Investigations can be initiated through intelligence, complaints from concerned citizens, surveillance, use of informants, infiltration, buy operations, and wiretaps or even by a routine traffic stop that results in the seizure of drugs or currency.

8.3 Intelligence

The gathering and analysis of information is central to every drug investigation. At the local level this intelligence can be provided by complaints made by concerned citizens, by interrogations of prisoners, by observations of investigators at narcotics-prone locations, by frequency and location of narcotics arrests, by checking on the prior arrests of suspects to determine if they had codefendants, by uniformed patrol officers who may be familiar with the area, or by confidential informants.

8.4 Citizen Complaints

At the street or local level, drug sales will attract the attention of residents and merchants, who observe increased suspicious activities in the neighborhood. Many of these persons will call the local police department to complain about these drug sales and about the corresponding increase in other crime as well. In areas with a dedicated narcotics investigation unit, detectives should investigate these complaints, with an eye toward initiating a case aimed at climbing the ladder of this criminal enterprise.

The prompt and thorough interview of complainants is essential; based on the nature and extent of their information and cooperation, a search warrant may be obtained for a particular location. If the complainants' information is insufficient or their cooperation is lacking, the investigators should seek a vantage point from which they may covertly observe the alleged activities.

8.5 Surveillance to Initiate Investigations

If the alleged drug sales are taking place on the street in public view, the investigators should document the activities, including license plate numbers, descriptions, and times of day, preferably using video or still cameras to capture these transactions. There are several possible results for the positive observation by the investigators of drug transactions: (1) Based on the investigators' expertise (prior experience) and quality of the observation, there may be probable cause to make an arrest; (2) a street-level "buy and bust" operation may be scheduled for another day, during which an investigator will make covert observations of drug sales and communicate the description of the buyers and perhaps their vehicles to other investigative team members, who will wait for the buyers to leave the area before arresting them, and at the end of the operation the seller is arrested and charged with the multiple sales; or (3) send an undercover police officer to attempt to make a purchase from the seller. In the first and second scenarios, all of the defendants should be advised of their Miranda rights and interrogated if a waiver is obtained. Aside from attempting to obtain a confession and gather intelligence, the investigator should assess the defendant as a possible confidential informant, thus allowing for the potential to ascend to the next step on the ladder. In the third scenario, the undercover police officer may be used as the basis for a "buy and bust," or the sale may be documented and the undercover officer may be allowed to return on another occasion to make a second buy and perhaps begin to work his or her way up the ladder to the next level.

8.6 Registered Confidential Informants

Unquestionably, confidential informants are used more in narcotics investigations than in all other types of investigation combined. There is a distinction between a confidential informant, a concerned citizen, and someone who an investigator may use as a regular source of information. Confidential informants, or CIs, are persons who are willing to impart their knowledge of an ongoing criminal enterprise to a law enforcement investigator on a continuing basis. Their motivations may include a deal with prosecutors regarding an existing criminal case, financial gain, revenge, community concerns, etc. Whatever their reasons for cooperating, they do so with the expectation that their identities will remain anonymous. While the courts have recognized the need to use confidential informants, a judge will sometimes issue an order requiring the release of the CI's true identity. That being the case, the best an investigator can do is to assure potential CI's that everything possible within the law will be done to protect their identities.

As an investigator you will not have the authority to make any promises with respect to a pending prosecution or plea arrangement. Rather, you should seek to establish good working relationships within your prosecutor's office so that consideration may be given to your recommendations. You will also be dealing with these same prosecutors in the event that your CI's information results in applications for wiretaps, search or arrest warrants, or presentations to a grand jury.

Prior to approaching a prosecutor on behalf of a potential CI's, you should fully evaluate his or her potential and risk. A complete background investigation and debriefing is required to learn the extent of the person's knowledge of the criminal network and the person's ability to introduce undercover officers into it. A prosecutor will not be inclined to make a deal unless the potential CI is able to produce a case that results in arrests of higher-level members, a significant number of arrests, or large seizures.

Once the background investigation and debriefing are completed, you should corroborate as much of the information as possible. Background checks should be conducted on all individuals identified by the potential CI and surveillances conducted of all locations that have been provided. You should now be aware of your potential CI's relatives, associates, and/or codefendants from prior arrests, girl- or boyfriends, employment history, education, present and former residences, vehicles used, driving history, history of drug use and any current or former treatments and rehabilitations, whether he/she has previously been registered as a CI, whether or not the person appears to be reliable, etc. Once you have accumulated this information, you can approach the prosecutor in an organized and informed manner. If the prosecutor concurs with your assessment and agrees to make a deal, the prosecutor will contact, or have you contact, the potential CI's attorney and arrange for a meeting at which the terms and conditions of any prosecutorial agreement will be discussed. If the potential CI and the prosecutor agree on these conditions, you are almost ready to begin operations.

If your potential CI is not currently a defendant in a criminal case but is, rather, a concerned citizen, someone offering to work for financial gain, or someone out for revenge, it will not be necessary to gain the approval of the prosecutor's office, unless of course you are an investigator employed by the prosecutor. Yet you should still conduct the same diligent background and corroborative investigation as described earlier. As an investigator in charge of CI's, it is imperative that you understand the motivations of your informants. Needless to say, even if the informants are not criminal defendants, they obviously have intimate knowledge of a criminal enterprise, or you would not be speaking to them. The mere fact that they are willing to provide you with information and access indicates that they are willing to manipulate others. Great care must be taken to ensure that they are not manipulating you, at least not without your knowledge. This same care should be taken whether the potential CI is a one-time informant, such as a girlfriend of a known dealer, or a potential long-term informant who will continue to operate within an organized criminal enterprise.

Registration procedures will vary from agency to agency, yet the concept remains the same. A file for each CI should be initiated. In addition to the information contained within the background and corroborative investigation, the file should contain a photograph of the CI, a description of any reward (judicial, financial, etc.), and a periodic review of his/her performance. If the CI is working for money, signed receipts should be obtained from the CI and retained within his/her file. For more information on the registration and ongoing supervision of informants it is recommended that investigators review *The Attorney General's Guidelines Regarding the Use of Confidential Informants,* which is periodically published by the U.S. government and which covers the use of confidential informants by all investigative agencies under the control of the Justice Department.

8.7 Handling Confidential Informants

As previously stated, each agency or department will have its own guidelines regarding the registration and management of CI's. In general, one investigator should be designated as the primary handler and one as the alternate, with both investigators being under the direct control of an investigative supervisor. All meetings with CI's should be conducted in the presence of at least one of these investigators (preferably the primary investigator); at all times, at least two investigators should be present. The identity of the CI should be restricted to investigators or members of the department or agency who have a need to know.

Regardless of his/her motivations, once a CI is registered, he or she becomes an "agent" of the police and his/her activities must be directed and monitored in such a way as to avoid the issue of entrapment. Entrapment can occur when any agent of the police encourages, persuades, induces, or otherwise motivates a person to engage in a criminal activity that the person would otherwise not have become involved with on his/her own.

Entrapment:

> In law, the instigation of a crime in the attempt to obtain cause for a criminal prosecution. Situations in which a government operative merely provides the occasion for the commission of a criminal act (e.g., when an undercover agent posing as a narcotics dealer is approached by a would-be customer) do not constitute entrapment. Only when the crime was not initially contemplated by the target is entrapment said to occur: thus, for example, an undercover agent may not recruit a previously law-abiding individual into a drug distribution ring in order to prosecute. Many police operations, especially in the areas of drugs and gambling, raise questions of entrapment, which is available as a defense in a trial.[*]

Merely providing someone with the opportunity to commit a crime is not entrapment, yet investigators need to guard against the use of coercion, threats, harassment, or pleas for sympathy made by a CI to an otherwise law-abiding person to convince that person to commit a crime. Naturally, the investigator will not be able to monitor the CI's activities around the clock, yet it should be cause for concern and further investigation if a CI produces a subject who has no prior criminal history.

Once your CI has been registered, you are ready to begin operations. Much like the director of a play or movie, the investigator in charge of a narcotics operation must have complete control. The narcotics industry is a violent business, and great care and planning are required to minimize the potential danger to undercover officers and CI's alike. CI's should never be treated as partners or equals; rather, their knowledge of the overall investigation should be limited to their immediate tasks. If more than one independent CI is being used in the same operation, their use and identities should not be disclosed to one another. Neither should CI's be forewarned of impending executions of search or arrest warrants or of the existence of court-ordered eavesdropping. Other than as part of an ongoing investigation, investigators should never socialize with CI's. Furthermore, CI's should have a clear understanding that their cooperation is in no way a free pass for them to commit other crimes, and they should be arrested immediately if there is probable cause to believe that they have.

8.8 Buy Operations

The "buy operation" is the basis for all ongoing narcotics investigations. As opposed to "buy and bust" operations, where the dealer is arrested after the sale, a "buy operation" is a long-term investigation designed to insert an undercover (UC) agent into the ongoing criminal enterprise, where he or she can purchase drugs from multiple dealers and hopefully work his/her way up the ladder. As the operation develops, it may be possible for the UC to introduce additional UC agents for the purpose of making purchases of larger quantities of drugs. Multiple "buys" are usually made from each seller as further evidence of their continued participation in the business of selling drugs.

No two "undercover buy operations" are exactly alike, but they all have at least one thing in common, an undercover agent. It is possible yet highly undesirable for a CI to act alone as the UC operative. As quickly as possible, the CI should introduce an undercover police officer into the operation. Once a UC police officer has been introduced, he or she will be able to work in conjunction with the CI until such time as the UC operative becomes accepted on his or her own merits. When the CI is no longer needed, he or she should be removed from that part of the investigation and directed to other areas.

Most "buy operations" that are conducted are quick investigations in which the UC operative meets with a seller, makes a buy, and then leaves the area. The UC operatives will return to their own lives at the end of the working day. There are also long-term "deep cover" operations, in which the UC will assume a full-time roll, including a fictional but well-documented identity. Generally, these types of long-term investigations are conducted on the federal level or by large departments with considerable resources to infiltrate organized crime. These investigations include direction from the U.S. Attorneys Office or local prosecutor, with the understanding that it will include the possibility that certain crimes will be committed or abetted by the UC operative. This is a recognized evil, but the ground rules must first be coordinated with the prosecutor's office before inserting a UC agent.

Prior to sending a UC operative to make a "buy," a complete "backup" plan must be established, taking into consideration the manpower necessary to cover the physical site, or "set," at which the buy is to be made. The safety of the UC operative is the foremost consideration, so the exact location of the UC agent at all times must be given the highest priority. All of the backup officers should be familiar with the location, including all entrances, stairways, elevators, basements, and roofs, the layout of the apartment or building, roadways, and traffic patterns (e.g., one-way streets, highway entrances/exits). A "preoperation" briefing should be held between the UC agent and the entire backup team to coordinate the positions of the backup team members; place parameters on the movements of the UC agent; and develop "key words" or hand signals to be used by the UC agent if he or she needs assistance; to agree on a postbuy surveillance; to ensure that the UC operative is not followed from the "set"; and to agree on a prearranged time and place to meet in the event that the UC operative does become separated from the "backup" team.

Whenever possible, the UC operative should be equipped with a hidden transmitter and recording device. While federal law permits the recording of conversations when the recording person is a party to it, some states require the consent of all parties. Know your law with respect to recording conversations. Videotape surveillance should also be maintained of the UC operative when he or she is in public view; especially when in the company of the seller, because there is no expectation of privacy in public places.

The UC operative should be provided with sufficient currency that has been photocopied or whose serial numbers have been otherwise recorded. Once the UC operative or UC operative and CI leave the prebuy briefing for the "set," they should be under the constant surveillance of the "backup" team until they reach the buy location. If the "buy" will take place in public view, the surveillance should be maintained throughout, including the return to the "postbuy" debriefing. If the "buy" is to take place indoors, the backup team should then take up their preassigned positions and await the exit of the UC operative or UC operative and CI.

"Buys" should be made at the predetermined location, and the UC agent should make every effort not to become mobile and leave that location for an unknown destination. In the event that the UC operative does leave with the seller, it is advisable for the operative to use his or her own vehicle. In planning for such contingencies, it is recommended that a GPS device be installed in the UC operative's vehicle prior to leaving for the set; in the absence of a GPS device, a GPS cellular phone should be in the possession of the UC operative at all times.

Surveillance by the backup team is essential when the UC operative is mobile. In the absence of GPS, visual contact must be maintained. Different vehicular surveillance tactics can be utilized, depending on the number of vehicles in the backup team. "Leapfrogging" or a "handoff" can be done with as few as two vehicles that will trade places with one another as the surveillance continues. If more vehicles are involved, other vehicles may be able to travel on parallel roads, periodically getting ahead of the subject vehicle and switching in and relieving the vehicles that are maintaining visual contact. If many vehicles are involved, it is possible to create a box around the subject vehicle by surrounding it, front, side, and rear, and switching vehicles and vehicle positions periodically. It is also possible that the backup team knows the ultimate destination and dispatches one or two vehicles ahead of the subject vehicle so that they arrive first and can take up a good position.

At all times while the UC operative is on the set, the backup teams must maintain a constant vigil, paying particular attention for lookouts or for accomplices of the seller. Once the UC operative has exchanged money with the seller for the drugs, the "buy" has been completed and the operative should leave the "set" as soon as possible for the prearranged meeting with the "backup" team. If the "buy" was made with the assistance of a CI, the CI should be debriefed separately and should not become a party to the postbuy debriefing of the UC police officer. Remember, the CI is not a part of the "team," but, rather, a "tool," and as such his or her participation and knowledge should be kept to a minimum.

At the debriefing, the UC operative should provide the investigator in charge of the buy operation with complete descriptions of the sellers, all other persons present during the sale, and a complete synopsis of any pre- and postbuy conversations with the CI, seller, and anyone else that was present. The UC operative should provide the investigator in charge with any recordings made. The investigator should make a duplicate copy of the recording for transcription purposes and should voucher the original for safekeeping, taking care to disable further recording capabilities on whatever type of media was used to record. The initials of both the CI and the investigator should be placed on the media, along with the case number and the date.

The UC operative and the investigating officer should prepare chronological reports documenting all aspects of the "buy," specifically including the name and a description of the seller and all others who were present. If a CI was used, the CI should be referred to by the registration number only. Additional reports should be prepared by any member of the "backup team" who made independent observations that are pertinent to the case, including descriptions and locations of "lookouts, other sellers, other buyers, vehicles, etc. It is advisable to record the license plates of all vehicles in the vicinity of the "buy location" and to determine to whom they are registered. Background checks should be conducted of all persons identified as being on the "set." The names of all individuals should be entered into the case intelligence file.

Proper documentation, handling, and laboratory analysis are necessary for every "buy." Many "testing kits" are commercially available that can be used in the field to confirm the presence of specific drugs. It is advisable to "field test" drugs prior to submitting them to the laboratory for quantitative and qualitative analysis, and any such testing should be done by the UC operative in the presence of at least one other member of the investigative team. If the drug was field tested by the UC operative in the presence of the seller at the time of the buy, it will not be necessary to "field test" it again. To maintain proper chain of custody over the drugs, they should remain in the possession of the UC operative at all times prior to the UC operative's delivering them to the police lab. As with any other evidence, the number of people involved in the chain of evidence should be kept to a minimum.

At the laboratory, qualitative and quantitative examinations should be requested so that both the presence and the purity of the drug can be determined. The purity is important in drugs that are susceptible to being "hit," or "stepped on (diluted)," such as heroin and cocaine. Drugs of a higher purity can be an indicator of the seller's position on the organizational ladder, with the most pure being at the top and the most diluted being at the street level.

Once all of the evidence has been properly documented, vouchered, or delivered to the laboratory for analysis, the tapes (if any) transcribed, and additional investigation, intelligence, and report writing completed, the planning for the next step can begin. It may be a plan to make another buy from the same seller or to try and "up-buy" to a larger quantity of drugs, hoping that will lead to a seller higher up on the ladder, which may or may not require the insertion of a second UC operative, or to make a purchase from another seller on the same step of the ladder. Other investigative possibilities include the application for a search warrant, court-ordered wiretap, or eavesdropping order. These orders can be applied for if the investigation has documented that the sellers use the telephone or other electronic equipment, including computers, to conduct illicit business. This documentation can include phone calls or e-mails between the UC operative or the CI and the seller, where the content includes the purchase of drugs, or by observations made by the UC operative, the CI, other investigators, or other reliable persons who have observed the seller using the telephone or other electronic device to conduct business.

The court-ordered wiretap/eavesdropping investigation will require significant training, manpower, and resources. Each investigator who monitors these conversations must be aware of the legal requirements in his/her jurisdiction. Generally speaking, only those conversations in which the seller is involved and conducting illicit business can be recorded. The conversations not involving crimes or in which the subject of the wiretap is not involved can only be periodically monitored to determine if the topic of the conversation has switched to crime or if the subject has now come on the line and is conducting illicit business. Court-ordered wiretaps can be amended if information becomes available indicating that others are also using the phone or electronic device to conduct illicit business. It is also possible to obtain court orders for public phones or payphones; yet again, there are restrictions on whose calls may be monitored and recorded.

The need for manpower is compounded by the transcription of the recorded telephone calls, surveillance of the subjects, surveillance during UC "buys," and surveillance of potential associates or other customers. Every license plate must be checked, every suspect backgrounded and cataloged in the intelligence file, every telephone number identified, etc. These investigative steps may lead to additional wiretap orders, seizures, and arrests. Operations of this nature are usually staffed 24 hours a day unless the court order directs otherwise, and they should not be undertaken with fewer than three investigators per shift, one to monitor the wiretap and two to conduct surveillance.

Whether or not your investigation is beginning, ending, moving up the ladder, or moving sideways, each and every step must be carefully planned, monitored, and documented. Once the current operation is brought to a close by arrests and seizures, the process of interviewing and evaluating the defendants with an eye towards "flipping" them as CI's must begin again.

Sex Crime Investigations

9

When ordinary citizens think of a sex crime, they first envision a forcible rape of a woman or a child. The real-life investigation of sex-related crimes is not so simple, because force is not always an element and women and children are not always the victims. Since each state's criminal laws differ with respect to language and penalties, this book will use the definitions set forth in the FBI's *Uniform Crime Reports*.

9.1 Sex Crime Definitions*

Sex Offenses — Forcible: Any sexual act directed against another person, forcibly and/or against that person's will; or not forcibly or against the person's will where the victim is incapable of giving consent.

A. *Forcible Rape:* The carnal knowledge of a person, forcibly and/or against that person's will; or not forcibly or against the person's will where the victim is incapable of giving consent because of his/her temporary or permanent mental or physical incapacity (or because of his/her youth).

B. *Forcible Sodomy:* Oral or anal sexual intercourse with another person, forcibly and/or against that person's will; or not forcibly against the person's will where the victim is incapable of giving

---

* National Incident-Based Reporting System Edition of the Uniform Crime Reporting Program.

consent because of his/her youth or because of his/her temporary or permanent mental or physical incapacity.

C. Sexual Assault with an Object: The use of an object or instrument to unlawfully penetrate, however slightly, the genital or anal opening of the body of another person, forcibly and/or against that person's will; or not forcibly or against the person's will where the victim is incapable of giving consent because of his/her youth or because of his/her temporary or permanent mental or physical incapacity.

D. Forcible Fondling: The touching of the private body parts of another person for the purpose of sexual gratification, forcibly and/or against that person's will; or not forcibly or against the person's will where the victim is incapable of giving consent because of his/her youth or because of his/her temporary or permanent mental incapacity.

Sex Offenses — Nonforcible: Unlawful, nonforcible sexual intercourse.

A. Incest: Nonforcible sexual intercourse between persons who are related to each other within the degrees wherein marriage is prohibited by law.

B. Statutory Rape: Nonforcible sexual intercourse with a person who is under the statutory age of consent.*

You will note the lack of gender reference in these definitions, yet many state criminal statutes will specifically include a description of a penis entering the vagina in forcible rape, obviously and intentionally eliminating males as victims of this specific crime. Yet these same statutes will include the penetration of the anus or mouth by a penis, fingers, or other objects when describing forcible sodomy. Simply stated, in states with such language in their criminal laws, only males can commit forcible rape, while both males and females can commit or be victims of forcible sodomy, touching, etc.

The second item of interest in the *Uniform Crime Reports* definitions is that not all sex crimes require the use of force. This theory is also consistent in state statutes, but the wording and age limits will vary. As in other parts of this book, you are urged to become familiar with your local laws!

Federal Register, April 29, 1994, Vol. 59, No. 82; *Federal Register*, November 1, 1999, Vol. 64, No. 210.

9.2 Forcible Sex Crimes

Human sexuality includes many acts that may in and of themselves be viewed as deviant or, depending on the jurisdiction, even as illegal. It is not the purpose of this book to discuss the issues of consensual acts of sodomy between members of the same sex or persons of the opposite sex, be they married, casual acquaintances, or strangers. The focus of this section is the investigation of forcible sex acts on human beings.

What constitutes force? Generally speaking, the force necessary to commit a sex crime can be physical, threatened, or implied. It is not necessary for a physical injury to be inflicted on the victim; rather, the mere implication that an injury will occur unless the victim cooperates is sufficient. The lack of consent by the victim is the basis for every forcible sex crime investigation and prosecution.

What constitutes consent? Consent is a conscious voluntary decision made by an adult person who is in full control of his/her mentality. Sexual decisions based on free will cannot be the basis for a forcible sex crime prosecution. Consent cannot be given by anyone who is a minor or anyone who is forced, threatened, mentally ill, drugged, or unconscious or by a person who is fraudulently touched in a sexual manner by a medical or other professional.

Who commits forcible sex crimes? Studies conducted by the legal, medical, psychological, and sociological communities have convincingly shown that persons who are known to the victims commit the majority of forcible sex crimes. These known perpetrators can be relatives, friends, coworkers, neighbors, schoolmates, medical, and religious persons, etc. While the percentages vary from study to study, stranger-on-stranger sex crimes rarely approach the 50% level. This was not always the case, because "stranger" rapes far outpaced acquaintance sex crimes throughout the years when these statistics were compiled. It is doubtful that acquaintance crimes have increased that dramatically; rather, it is more likely that the shame associated with the reporting of such crimes to the police has diminished or that certain groups have developed better reporting strategies.

9.3 Are Sex Crimes about Sex?

It has long been an accepted principle among members of the psychiatric, psychological, and sociological communities that rape and other forcible sex crimes have nothing to do with passion, lust, love, or physiological urges to reproduce; rather, they are about dominance, deviance, and control. Take, for example, the following quote from the National Center for Victims of Crime:

If an individual is sexually assaulted:

It is important that the victim of sexual assault understand that no matter where they were, the time of day or night assaulted, what they were wearing, or what they said or did, if they did not want the sexual contact, then the assault was in no way their fault. Persons who commit sexual assault do so out of a need to control, dominate, abuse, and humiliate. Sexual assault is the articulation of aggression through sex, and has little to do with passion, lust, desire, or sexual arousal.*

Investigators will be well served to keep this in mind when developing theories and profiles about both unknown and known perpetrators. For example, studies have shown that the recidivism rate for a convicted rapist is significantly higher than the rates of other criminals when it comes to committing the same type of crime. A study by the Office of Justice Programs revealed the following:

Rearrest for a new sex crime:

Compared to non-sex offenders released from state prisons, released sex offenders were four times more likely to be rearrested for a sex crime. Within the first 3 years following their release from prison in 1994, 5.3% (517 of the 9,691) of released sex offenders were rearrested for a sex crime. The rate for the 262,420 released non-sex offenders was lower, 1.3% (3,328 of 262,420).

The first 12 months following their release from a state prison was the period when 40% of sex crimes were allegedly committed by the released sex offenders.†

This should not eliminate other suspects who have never been arrested or those who have been arrested for crimes other than forcible sex, yet it will

---

* National Center for Victims of Crime, Violence Against Women, Sexual Assault, http://www.ncvc.org/ncvc/Main.aspx
† U.S. Department of Justice, Office of Justice Programs, Bureau of Justice Statistics. *Recidivism of Sex Offenders Released from Prison in 1994*, November 2003, NCJ 198281.

be beneficial for investigators to monitor the "sex offender" registries that are now available.

9.4 Investigating Forcible Nonstranger Sex Crimes

When investigating allegations of a forcible sex crime by an assailant who is personally known to the complainant, the issues surrounding the incident may be somewhat less clear than those involving the stereotypical "stranger" rapist. Investigators assigned to specialized sex crimes units will generally receive "sensitivity" training so that they can relate to and understand the psychological trauma that is experienced by victims. There is also considerable psychological trauma inflicted on those who are wrongfully accused. As an investigator it is your responsibility to keep an open mind, avoiding any outside pressures from gender-related support groups or biases that may have been developed during your own life experiences. Not every victim will have cuts and bruises, and not every complainant will be telling the truth.

The relationship between complainant and the accused will run the gamut, from those between relatives, including husband and wife, to those who are just the most casual of acquaintances.

9.5 Spousal Offenses

Once exempted from the sex crimes laws, spousal rape is now a crime throughout the entire country, but, again, these laws will vary from state to state. The relationship between a husband and wife is very complex, both emotionally and legally, and if it has reached the stage where one or the other has reported a forcible sex act, there are likely to be other issues that plague that relationship as well. As the investigator in this type of case, you may become aware of other problems and indicators, such as pending or anticipated divorce or separation, child custody issues, monetary problems, infidelity, and prior physical assaults. If there is no independent corroborating evidence such as injuries or witnesses, the investigator must rely on interviews of parties, their relatives, friends, and acquaintances. DNA evidence should be collected. But remember that evidence of a sexual encounter between a husband and wife is not in and of itself proof of a crime. The real issue in this type of case is whether or not there was "consent."

Remember, too, that Miranda warnings are not required so long as the person being questioned is not in custody or made to feel that he or she is not free to leave.

It is through multiple, thoughtful interviews of both parties that the investigator may be able to discover the facts. The reason for more than one interview of the parties involved is to explore and expand on previously provided information, to observe reactions to claims by the other party, and to uncover discrepancies with previous interviews. Unlike a "stranger" rape, there is usually no issue of flight by the spouse. So unless there are other reasons of urgency, e.g., the potential for further assault, or other corroborating evidence, it is recommended that the investigator proceed with caution; and prior to making an arrest, the investigator should consult with the prosecutor assigned to this matter.

9.6 Acquaintance Sex Crimes

The reporting of this type of allegation will vary from the immediate, such as being overheard screaming, running, and fighting back, to calls to the police or rape hotlines within minutes, hours, days, or weeks or even months later.

As with most other crimes, the investigator will generally not be the first officer on the scene. In cases where the crime has just occurred, the first officer should have interviewed or attempted to interview the complainant to get the basic facts, safeguarded the crime scene, requested or confirmed the response of an ambulance, identified and segregated any witnesses, and notified the detective unit.

Regardless of the relationship between the complainant and the accused or the timeliness of reporting, the investigator must ensure that a complete and thorough investigation is completed in every instance, including the safeguarding and processing of the crime scene if it still exists, the collection of evidence, including rape kit evidence at the hospital if still applicable, photographs and/or video of the victim's wounds or bruises, and thoughtful interviewing of the complainant, the accused, and any and all witnesses.

Many acquaintance crimes will occur within a residence or temporary lodging facility, such as a hotel or motel. When processing this type of scene, investigators should keep in mind that bedding materials, towels, washcloths, victim's and suspect's clothing, etc., might contain hair or bodily fluids and secretions from which DNA evidence may be obtained to identify its donor. There may also be DNA present from other individuals. If the evidence is being collected from the residence of the complainant, it is imperative for the investigator to learn the identities of all persons with whom the complainant had consensual sexual relations. The same holds true for the residence of the accused, for at the very least it may provide additional persons to interview regarding the suspect's personal and sexual habits. Investigators must always evaluate the need for obtaining a search warrant to ensure that any evidence obtained will be useful during a prosecution.

When available, DNA evidence will be invaluable in all cases where the alleged perpetrator denies having sexual relations with the complainant. However, in acquaintance cases it not uncommon for the accused to admit to "consensual" sex with the complainant. As with marital cases, acquaintance investigations will focus on the issue of consent.

9.7 Sex Crimes, Alcohol, and Drugs

Acquaintance and "date rapes" often involve the use of alcohol, drugs, or both. The consumption of these drugs may be either voluntary or unknowingly administered to the complainant. Drugs and alcohol are usually a component of sex crimes that occur among college students, because much of their new social life revolves around fraternity/sorority parties, college bars, etc.

Cases involving the voluntary taking of drugs and/or alcohol by the complainant will be the hardest for a prosecutor to prove in court, unless of course other facts can be shown to indicate that the accused somehow denied the victim the ability to withhold consent or knew that the victim was unable to give consent. One such example would be if the accused were aware that the complainant had lost consciousness prior to engaging in sexual relations. Another example may occur if it can be shown that the accused induced the complainant to consume enough drugs or alcohol to the point of becoming disorientated, thereby making it impossible for the complaint to resist. This type of information will generally come from direct interviews of the accused or of others, who may be able to document past occasions where the accused had done the same thing to others.

Some victims may withhold information regarding their own voluntary intoxication because they may perceive them as being a contributing factor to the assault, or they may be embarrassed for fear of looking bad either to the investigator or to the victim's own family. Investigators must assure these individuals that they will not get into trouble for voluntarily drinking or taking drugs, either with or before their meeting with the suspect but, rather, that the real trouble will take place if this information is first revealed at a trial.

On the other hand, the intentional surreptitious administration of alcohol or the "date-rape" drugs gamma hydroxybutyrate (GHB) and flunitrazepam (Rohypnol) or any other drug that can cause disorientation or a lowering of inhibitions will leave no doubt that the complainant was unable to request consent. Therefore, it is recommended that in addition to use of the rape kit, investigators should request blood and urine samples for toxicological examination in these cases whenever possible.

9.8 Interviewing the Victim — Nonstranger Assaults

Sex crime investigators are usually not the first law enforcement officers to speak with the complainant. As with most other crimes, a uniformed officer is likely to have responded first, spoken with the complainant, given aid to and/or requested an ambulance for the victim, secured the crime scene, made an arrest, transmitted an alarm, and segregated any witnesses. It is also quite likely that the victim has spoken with medical personal, counselors, friends, and relatives before speaking with the investigator.

As the investigator, it would be helpful to interview the responding police officer or any other professional or individual who may have spoken with the victim prior to your interview, such as a doctor, nurse, sex crime advocate, priest, relative, or friend, so as to gain a clearer picture of the events at the scene and the statements of the complainant and any witnesses.

In nonstranger cases it is likely that the complainant possesses sufficient information regarding the identity and whereabouts of the accused to enable the investigator to locate the individual. Since the "who" is no longer a major factor, the focus of the interview will be on the "what, when, where, why, and how."

At all times during the initial interview the investigator must keep in mind the emotional condition of the complainant. Universally, victims of sex crimes experience a loss of control over their lives and bodies and may have feelings of guilt, fear, responsibility, or shame. They will also have a fear of the unknown or of what awaits them in the criminal justice arena.

The actions and demeanor of the investigator can have a profound effect on the future cooperation of the complainant in prosecuting this case. With this in mind, the investigator should be supportive, sympathetic, reassuring, and informative when conducting this initial interview. Empowering and gaining the trust of the complainant is of great importance. The complainant should be allowed to make as many decisions as possible so that he/she may begin to feel that he/she is back in control of his/her life. For example, it may be beneficial to allow the complainant to decide when and where to conduct the interview, so long as there is no compelling reason to conduct it immediately. The victim should be allowed to decide whether or not a third party, such as a relative, friend, or sex assault advocate, should be present, so long as their presence is not disruptive to the investigation.

It is advisable to make the complainant as comfortable as possible within the immediate surroundings. The victim should never be placed in a corner, nor should the investigator position him-/herself in too close proximity so as to violate the victim's "personal space," because this may limit the control that he/she is trying to regain over his/her life. Touching the victim should be avoided unless he/she has requested it and the investigator feels comfortable giving the victim "a shoulder to cry on." It is advisable that at least one other person be present during any such physical contact with the victim.

Prior to questioning, the investigator should clearly inform the complainant of the investigator's function, which is to find and corroborate the facts surrounding the assault so that there can be a successful prosecution. The victim should be allowed and encouraged to ask questions prior to the interview. Victims may be disoriented, confused, frightened, hostile, or non-emotional, yet the investigator must maintain a professional and supportive attitude. Any hostility shown by the complainant should be redirected toward the ultimate goal of arresting and prosecuting the perpetrator, by reassuring the victim that you are there to help, that you are on his/her side, that you feel bad about what happened, and that the questions you are about to ask are a necessary part of a successful prosecution. If the investigator can make the complainant feel as if they are a team with a common sense of purpose, it will set the proper tone for the future.

The victim should be allowed to relate his/her story at his/her own pace, without unnecessary interruptions for clarifications, so long as the person does not stray too far from the main issues. It is advisable to encourage the victim to tell his/her story in a narrative fashion, from beginning to end, without interruption. Detailed note taking is not necessary during this stage of the interview, because it can actually have a negative impact on the interview. It is sufficient to jot down key points to which you wish to return, yet give your full attention to the victim. In cases where the victim is unable or unwilling to provide a running narrative, the investigator should use short, open-ended questions that relate to the instant information the victim was supplying, such as "And what happened next?" or "What did he say next?" These questions should never be accusatory or judgmental.

It is appropriate for the investigator to take advantage of natural pauses in the victim's narration, especially those that occur when the individual is moving from one segment of the story to the next, to review parts of the segment with the victim. This will allow the investigator to seek clarification of any issues. At the same time it will provide a mirror to the victim by which to see his/her story through your eyes. Again, this should not be in-depth questioning that disrupts the victim's narrative, but a short clarification break that will demonstrate to the victim that you are listening.

While listening to the victim, the investigator must identify any information that may be corroborated by witnesses or by such independent means as date-/time-stamped receipts for garage parking, convenience stores, restaurant bills, motels, etc. While these issues do not have anything to do with "consent," they will be useful in verifying the victim's timeline.

The relationship between the complainant and the victim may be remote or intimate. It is important during this initial interview for the investigator to identify the type and depth of this relationship, because it will shape the focus of the investigation. In cases where there is no prior history of a close or intimate relationship, the investigator will need to document the events that led up to the assault. In cases where there was a prior or continuing intimate relationship, the investigator will need to identify the nature and frequency of this relationship and pay special attention to the victim's lack of or withdrawal of consent. In some cases it may be as simple as documenting the physical injuries sustained by the victim, while in others the investigator may become involved in interpreting a very complex interpersonal relationship between long-term partners.

Once the victim has finished the initial narration, the investigator should have the benefit of having learned about the incident from the first officer, medical personnel, social worker/sex crime advocate, friends or relatives of the victim, and the victim himself/herself. With this in mind, the investigator should look for any inconsistencies in the information and seek clarification with follow-up questions during the remaining part of the initial interview. You may find that the victim described the crime of rape to you yet failed to mention an act of oral or anal sodomy that was previously disclosed to the doctor or nurse. This may be as simple as embarrassment on the part of the victim, but it is the type of discrepancy that must be cleared up immediately. The victim must be informed that the sexual assault may include multiple criminal charges against the perpetrator and that you must identify each specific crime or the number of times the same crime was committed so that multiple counts of the same charge may be brought against the defendant. There may also be discrepancies in the time or sequence of events. Yet while it is not uncommon for victims of sex crimes to be confused, the investigator must be aware of the existence of any discrepancies that need to be clarified.

As discussed earlier, the victim may also leave out actions on his/her own part that he/she is embarrassed about or which he/she feels may have contributed to the assault, such as the voluntary use of drugs and a prior consensual sexual experience with the accused. Questions regarding these issues should be explained to the victim so that they do not appear accusatory but, rather, as necessary to proving the case. The victim should be made aware that the criminal defense may raise such issues at trial, so it is important for the prosecution to be aware of these actions beforehand rather than being surprised at trial. If the victim does reveal any such behaviors, it is important for the investigator to assure the victim that these behaviors in no way contributed to the use of force by the accused.

These clarifying questions should not be asked one after the other, for to do so may give the impression that the investigator does not believe the complainant. Using the victim's narrative as a guide, these questions should be worked into the interview in the appropriate places.

During the victim's narration, the investigator will have had the opportunity to take note of the language used by the victim to describe sexual acts,
body parts, people, etc. It is important for the investigator to relate to the
victim and "speak his/her language," yet any slang words or jargon must be
clarified. For example, "When you say he forced you to give him a "blow job,"
you mean that he made you take his penis into your mouth?"

After this type of clarification it would be appropriate for the investigator
to use the term "blow job" during the remaining interview. On the other
hand, the investigator should always use correct anatomical descriptions
unless the victim uses slang or jargon first. Many times minors/children will
have their own personal "pet names" for their body parts or those of the
opposite sex. It is up to the investigator to determine and record the correct
meaning of these "pet words," such as asking the child "Can you point to
your 'ding-ding'?"

For the purpose of reporting, the exact words of the victim should be
used and not sanitized, e.g., "Then he stuck his dick into my cunt" should
be recorded in the report rather than "The victim stated that the perpetrator
then placed his penis into her vagina."

During this second phase of the interview the investigator should be
looking to verify the legal elements necessary to charge an individual with
a sexual crime, particularly the type of force (physical, threatened, use of
coercion, use of date-rape drugs, etc.), the nature of the sex act(s), and the
number of counts to be considered, e.g., multiple instances of penile/vag-
inal penetrations.

As with any criminal investigation, the investigator should document the
following during the interview:

1. How the victim and the suspect arrived at and exited from crime
   scene.
2. The relationship between the victim and suspect. Any prior sexual
   history, consensual or forced.
3. The identity, residence, employment, family, etc., of the suspect.
4. The physical description of the suspect, including birthmarks, tattoos,
   circumcision, warts, or any deformities in areas of the body that are
   not plainly visible, such as the genitals.
5. The actions of the suspect while with the victim prior to, during, and
   after the assault.
6. The actions of the victim prior to, during, and after the assault,
   including the amount of time between the assault and the report.
7. The nature of the force, threat of force, or coercion used by the
   suspect.
8. The nature of the denial of consent by the complainant.

9. The use of drugs administered to the victim by the suspect to render the victim unable to give consent.
10. Were any objects used by the suspect during the assault?
11. Were any other crimes committed in addition to the sexual assault?
12. Are there any witnesses or other corroborating evidence that the complainant is aware of?
13. Did the suspect use any of the victim's clothing, towels, or other material to clean up with after the assault?
14. Has the victim bathed or douched prior to the medical examination?
15. Has the complainant seen the suspect since the assault?
16. Has the complainant had sexual relations with anyone, including the suspect, within a day before or after the assault?
17. Obtain photographs of all wounds and bruises.

Once the initial interview is completed, the investigator should provide the complainant with an overview of the remaining investigation and prosecution processes. The complainant should be told that the investigator would continue to seek evidence that can corroborate the elements of the crime(s) that could be charged, including the interviewing of witnesses, and the suspect. The investigator should address any issues of personal safety and take the necessary steps to ensure that no further harm comes to the complainant. The complainant should also be told that the investigator will be in contact with him/her and that it is not uncommon to conduct follow-up interviews with complainants, both before and after an arrest.

9.9 Interviewing the Suspect — Nonstranger Assaults

It is recommended that the initial interview of the suspect in cases where the complainant and suspect are known to each other be conducted as soon as possible after the complaint is made. Even though you may have established the "probable cause" necessary to make an arrest based on the complainant's statements and any medical or other corroborating evidence, you should not make an arrest at this time unless there is some compelling reason to do so, e.g., the safety of the complainant or the risk of flight of the suspect.

Surprise visits and interviews of the suspect will usually produce the best results. In nonstranger cases there is a possibility that the suspect will be unaware that the complainant has called the police, and therefore the suspect may not have prepared for the interview.

Remember, not all complainants tell the truth, nor is every suspect guilty. A complete and thorough investigation, including the interview of the suspect, should be conducted. Differentiation is made here between an "interview" and an "interrogation" of the suspect. During this initial interview of the suspect, the investigator should take great pains not to give the impression that the suspect is under arrest or not free to leave, thereby triggering the Miranda warnings. It is important for the investigator to gain the trust of the suspect or at least make the suspect understand that the investigator is conducting a full and unbiased investigation and is interested in hearing the suspect's recollection of the events.

9.10 Preparation for the Interviewing of Suspects

At this stage the investigator will have knowledge of the outcome of the crime scene search, although not all test results may have been obtained, and the benefit of the information provided by the complainant, witnesses, medical personnel, family, etc. To supplement this information, the investigator should conduct a complete background investigation of the suspect, including a complete pedigree, employment, residence, prior arrest record, and if possible physical and mental illnesses and treatments.

As with any other interview, the investigator should allow the suspect to narrate the story without constant interruptions, yet still maintaining control of the interview. The suspect should not be allowed to wander too far from the events leading up to, during, and after the alleged sexual assault. It is appropriate to refocus the suspect if the need arises by saying something like "Could you just go back to the part where you said …" or "So, you indicated that she finished her drink and smiled at you. What happened next?" It is always best to use opened-ended questions to help the suspect focus and continue with the narration.

It is a good technique to have the suspect observe you taking notes during his/her narration while at the same time making frequent eye contact with the suspect and nodding with encouragement. From this technique the suspect will get the impression that the investigator pays attention and takes good notes. This belief by the suspect will be beneficial in the second part of the interview, when the investigator begins to ask direct questions of the suspect and leafs through the investigator's notebook, pausing periodically as if to review certain facts that were related by the victim, witnesses, or notes from the crime scene.

During this second stage of the interview the investigator may choose to be more forceful and challenge the suspect's version either with real information or by bluffing. If the investigator chooses to use a bluff first, it should not be about a direct element of the alleged crime; instead, initial bluffs should begin with rather unimportant issues and the reaction of the suspect should be closely observed. For example, "John, I've already spoken with several sorority girls who've told me about you guys' spiking the rum punch to get them stoned." "John" may deny this, or he may tell you that he has spiked the punch in the past or that he actually spiked the punch that was consumed by the victim.

After the suspect has completed his initial narration of the story, the investigator should take a few moments to review his/her notes. During this period the investigator should give the appearance of reviewing notes from earlier events or interviews in the notepad or from another notepad altogether. If the investigator is aware of some real minor discrepancies between the suspect version and that of the complainant, now would be a good time to pose those questions. For example: "Okay John, you just told me that you had a date arranged with Mary last night for 7 P.M at the bar, but Mary doesn't get home from school until 10 P.M." This type of fact/question will put the suspect on the defensive, yet the suspect will also be aware that your notes contain facts that he/she is unaware of.

If the suspect acknowledges that he/she made a mistake or misspoke, it may be a good time for a meaningful bluff. For example, in a case where the victim alleges that she was drugged and could not give consent, the investigator may follow up with "So, we can agree that Mary didn't get to the bar until sometime after 10 P.M.? Right? John, are you aware that the bar recently installed surveillance cameras to keep an eye on the bartenders? That's right John, there is a videotape of you putting something into Mary's drink."

The investigator should keep in mind that this type of confrontational question may lead to the end of the interview. The suspect may feel so threatened by this line of questioning that he/she refuses to answer any further questions. On the other hand, the suspect may offer up a lie, such as "Oh that! That was just Sweet and Low," in which case the investigator should keep up the pressure with follow-up questions. Another possibility is that the suspect will confess.

In the event the suspect responds with reasonable explanations to either a contradiction of fact or a bluff, the investigator should continue to pose questions based on previous knowledge as well as on the narrative of the suspect. Again, detailed note taking is advisable at this stage, as is attention to minute details in the suspect's story, since the information obtained will need to be accurately recorded in the investigator's report and will also serve as the basis for follow-up interviews with the complainant and the suspect.

Once this suspect interview is completed, the investigator will have determined if an arrest will be made or if additional investigation will be required, including consultation with the prosecutor. If the investigation is to continue, the investigator must analyze both the complainant's and the suspect's versions of the events and timelines, keeping an eye open for contradictions, motives, and exculpatory or incriminating statements, and attempt to verify or disprove any open questions through independent means. Hopefully, the results of lab tests will be completed as well.

Armed with this analysis, and after pursuing any further investigative leads, the investigator should conduct a second interview of the complainant. By this time the complainant will have had sufficient time to reflect on the entire incident. But the investigator should understand that not all people react the same way to sexual assaults. You may find that the complainant is well adjusted or is withdrawn and suffering psychologically as a result of the assault. The investigator's demeanor must remain professional yet empathetic and reassuring if necessary.

During this second interview, the complainant should again be allowed to tell the story in a narrative manner, without unnecessary interruptions to answer the investigator's questions. During this segment of the interview the investigator should not be taking detailed notes but, rather, paying close attention to the story for any inconsistencies with the prior interview, with the suspect's version, or with the known independent facts.

After the complainant has retold the events, the investigator should explain to the complainant the adversarial nature of the criminal trial and let the complainant know that the defense attorney will be looking to discredit the complainant's testimony by any means possible. The investigator can now use this concept as the basis for asking direct follow-up questions, paying particular attention to any contradictions in the two complainant interviews as well as using any defenses or accusations raised by the suspect or the independent evidence. It is imperative that any inaccuracies, lies, ulterior motives, or detrimental or high risk behaviors in the complainant's story or past history be disclosed now rather than be a surprise at a trial.

Because each nonstranger case is different, the investigator may have developed enough evidence to make an arrest, continue with the investigation, or close the case as "unfounded," by "exceptional means," or administratively with no results, as described in the FBI's Uniform Crime Reporting program.

If an arrest is made, the defendant should be advised of his/her Miranda rights, followed by an interrogation if consent is given. If the investigation is to continue, it is advisable for the investigator to consult with the prosecutor prior to conducting a second interview with the suspect. The prosecutor may be able to provide the investigator with valuable insight and direction regarding the remaining investigation.

9.11 Stranger Sex Crimes

Once thought to be the most common type of sex-related crime, an attack by a complete stranger is now believed to account for a much smaller percentage of assaults as compared to those by known attackers. In fact, most studies, including those conducted by the U.S. Department of Justice, indicate that strangers committed only 20–30% of the reported sexual assaults.

The investigator will usually be notified by a uniformed officer that a rape has been reported. If the investigator is responding to the crime scene, he/she will need to interview the first officer and determine if the scene has been properly identified and secured, if any evidence has been identified, if there were any witnesses or arrests, and if a crime scene technician has been notified. It is a good idea for the investigator to take photographs of the scene as it appeared on his/her arrival. These photos will not take the place of crime scene photos, but they may become useful to work with as the investigation proceeds. Photos should also include all entrances and exits, potential hiding places, escape routes, etc.

In stranger assaults, the identity of the attacker becomes the primary focus of the investigation. The crime scene must be identified and processed in accordance with the previously discussed protocols, keeping in mind that there may be multiple crime scenes, including the victim herself/himself. Medical treatment for the victim is a primary concern, as is the collection of rape kit evidence and any materials that may have been used by the attacker to clean up after an assault. Even if the attacker did not clean up after the attack, trace evidence may be available on the victim's clothing, including bodily fluids, hairs, etc.

The lag time between the assault and the report will vary and is not within the investigator's control. Nonetheless, the crime scene(s) must be located and processed, even if weeks or months have passed since the attack. Even in cases where substantial periods of time have passed, the evidentiary value of fingerprints or DNA found in a location where the offender had no permission or authority to be will be substantial. If the crime scene is in a public place, it is still quite possible that this type of evidence will have value at a trial even if a great deal of time has passed between occurrence and report. Finally, any DNA and fingerprint evidence may provide the possibility of matching the same offender to other crime scenes.

9.12 Serial Crimes

The psychology of the rapist has been the subject of hundreds of independent and government-sponsored studies throughout history, and the overwhelming conclusion has been that rapes and related sex crimes have nothing to do with normal reproductive urges. It is widely accepted that these deviant aggressive acts are committed by people who suffer from a mental illness and that the use forced sexual acts is meant to demonstrate their power over another individual or serves as a release of anger or rage. The likelihood that this type of crime will be committed only once by this type of deranged person is quite remote. Therefore, it is reasonable for investigators to assume that most stranger rapists have committed similar crimes in the past and will likely continue to do so.

Every "stranger" sex crime investigation should begin with the premise that the offender has done this before. Therefore, investigators must pay particular attention to identifying and documenting minute details, including but not limited to the offender's physical characteristics, speech, body odors, and method of assault, the type of sexual or sadistic acts, and the offender's actions before, during, and after the assault. It may be possible to link sexual offenders to other crimes by recognizing an MO or some specific oddity, such as taking an earring as a trophy, biting or pinching the victim's genitals, leaving marks on the victim's body with a pen or lipstick, or making the victim repeat certain phrases. Issues of MO can include a vehicle that is used, a ski mask, the time of day of the assaults, the type of force, and the location and means of getting the victim there, e.g., follows the victim into an elevator, displays a pearl-handled revolver, takes victim to the rooftop.

Investigators who work in departments that have a dedicated sex crimes unit will likely have an easier time identifying pattern or serial sex offenders. These departments tend to be larger, well-funded agencies, and they may employ crime analysts and/or profilers as well. If you are an investigator who works in a smaller, less specialized, or underfunded department, it is recommended that after you conduct your initial investigation of a stranger sex crime, you review all previously reported sexual assaults within your jurisdiction as well as surrounding jurisdictions, keeping an eye open for similarities. You may also wish to seek the assistance of other law enforcement agencies, such as those of larger cities or states or the FBI, to help identify whether a pattern exists in your location, if you think a "profile" would help.

9.13 Victim Interview — Stranger Sex Crimes

Prior to interviewing the victim, it is good practice to complete the interview of the first officer; all witness interviews, and interviews of medical personnel or the victim's friends or relatives that may have been with him/her after the assault. It would also be helpful to have a good working knowledge of the crime scene, including the work photographs referred to earlier, which may come in handy during the victim interview.

The issues involved in interviewing the victim of a stranger sex crime can be substantially different from those involving known-offender cases. First, the victim will most likely not know the identity of the offender. Second, not only will the victim have experienced a sexual violation, but she/he may also have been subjected to a greater degree of physical force or threatened force than in nonstranger cases. Each person will react differently to being victimized in this manner, so investigators will need to be flexible and empathetic.

The trauma associated with this type of attack and the corresponding loss of control over one's physical being, may cause some victims to unconsciously block out certain aspects of the assault; others may intentionally choose not to relive the assault with the investigator. Investigators must be reassuring by letting the victim know that they feel bad about what happened to the victim and that their sole purpose is to catch the person who did it. The investigator should use discretion and allow the victim to decide if the interview should go forward immediately or if it should take place at a later date.

If the interview is to take place at a later time, it is imperative that the investigator instruct the victim to seek medical assistance, including the rape kit if it has not already been done, and to avoid bathing or cleaning prior to doing so, to avoid destruction of potential evidence. The investigator should also attempt to obtain any of the victim's clothing that was worn at the time of the attack as well as any items that were in contact with the offender.

If the interview is to go forward, the investigator should ensure that the victim is not closed in or made to feel intimidated in any way. Again, it is time for the investigator to practice the art of listening. To begin, the victim's attention should be directed to a point in time that preceded the assault when he/she was involved in normal activities. Once the victim begins to relate the events, the investigator should not interrupt the narration; rather, the victim should be urged to continue through the completion of the story. If there are natural pauses during this narration, the investigator can ask short, opened-ended review-type questions to get the victim started again, such as "You were saying that once he pushed you into the basement he took out a rope. What did he do next?" This will help the victim refocus and assure him/her that the investigator is actually listening.

Once the victim has related the entire story, the investigator can offer a brief review and begin to ask follow-up questions. As discussed earlier, minute details can have a dramatic effect on the outcome of these investigations. Since the offender's identity is central to the investigation, every aspect of the offender should be reviewed, including physical characteristics, clothing, accent, speech patterns, words and phrases used, the nature of the first encounter, e.g., a "blitz," or direct physical assault that incapacitated the victim, or a surprise attack using a knife or gun, or perhaps a "con," where the victim was lured into the situation, the type of physical force used or threatened, fetishes, sadistic acts, sexual acts, impotency, how the victim and the offender got to and left the crime scene if known, etc. It is also important to learn information about the victim as well, such as where he/she works or goes to school, education level, and any hobbies or special interests.

By the end of this interview, the investigator will have determined if the victim can identify the offender. If the answer if yes, the investigator should arrange for the victim to view photographs of potential suspects if such a central repository exists within the investigator's department. It would be best for the investigator to escort the victim to and from viewing.

The investigator should also inform the victim of the remaining investigative procedures, e.g., the possibility of returning to show the victim additional photographs, the potential for the viewing of physical lineups, and what to expect from the local criminal justice system in the event that an arrest is made.

9.14 Canvass

It is generally best to conduct a witness canvass in the vicinity of the crime scene after the victim and all known witnesses have been identified. To do so before these interviews may eliminate certain key information, such as a description of the offender's vehicle or the location of the preassault hiding place.

9.15 Case Analysis

Once the crime scene has been processed, all of the evidence, including the rape kit submitted for laboratory analysis, all interviews and canvass completed, and all investigative leads followed up on, it will be necessary for the investigator to analyze what has been learned. This case can then be compared to other attacks that have occurred in the same and surrounding areas. This task will become easier if DNA evidence is available and if it can be processed in a timely manner.

If a crime analyst is on staff, his/her assistance should be sought in an effort to determine if this case is part of a larger pattern. Such analysis may provide additional information and may even be a predictor of future assaults by demonstrating a pattern of crimes occurring on certain days of the week, at certain types of locations, or at certain times of day. If no analyst is available, the investigator may consider seeking the assistance of the FBI, as previously discussed.

Ultimately, the responsibility for following through with the case lies with the investigator. According to Vernon Geberth, discussing *investigative assessment*:

> The detective gathers information, attempts to reconstruct the incident, develops a theory about the incident, and then assesses these data to see whether or not the theory is consistent with the facts of the case. The investigators brainstorm the case during the investigative critique. They use their intuition, follow hunches, and make educated guesses based upon their extensive personal experience in homicide investigation.[*]

This same technique holds true for sex crime investigators as well.

[*] Vernon J. Geberth, , p. 502.

Arrest Strategies

10

Nowhere else in the field of law enforcement does a dichotomy exist such as that between the arrest situations faced by uniformed officers and those faced by detectives. The procedures taught to law enforcement officers in their respective academies are designed to prepare them to deal with the unexpected. Hand-to-hand combat, the use of batons, mace, and stun guns, and the use of deadly physical force are all taught to officers and continually reinforced during periodic training throughout their careers for the purpose of their personal protection, the protection of others, and the safe apprehension of prisoners. Beyond a doubt, the most difficult arrest situations are those that are routinely encountered by members of the uniformed patrol on a daily basis.

This is not to say that no risk is involved in arrests made as the result of an investigation. Quite the contrary, risk is always involved when dealing with violent persons or, for that matter, with any person that will be facing a loss of freedom. The advantage of the investigator in an arrest situation is simply the ability to plan the operation in advance.

Since most law enforcement detectives are "generalists," meaning they will handle all sorts of cases, from white-collar crimes to homicides, each arrest situation will be different. Some arrests can be made simply by inviting the future defendant into your office, such as a bookkeeper who has forged her boss's name on a series of petty cash checks; at other times you may have to stake out a bar or a residence and await the arrival of your target.

Other issues will come into play as well, such as whether or not an accusatory instrument has been filed with the court against the defendant. If you are in possession of an arrest warrant, you will be able to enter the defendant's abode to effect the arrest. On the other hand, if no such accusatory instrument or arrest warrant has been issued, you will not be able to enter the abode uninvited, yet you will not have given up your ability to attempt an interrogation. These choices are made by detectives on a case-by-case basis hundreds of times each day.

Whether you are acting with an arrest warrant or on probable cause developed through your investigative process, you have now reached the point of apprehension. The benefit that detectives have in effecting arrests is their general ability to orchestrate events. The following things must be considered at a minimum:

Nature of the crime: shoplifting or armed robbery?
Background: previous arrest reports; history of violent behavior
Arrest location: public place; inside residence; workplace
Elements of surprise and immobilization
Equipment/backup required
Number of persons to be arrested
Ingress/egress
Transportation

10.1 Nature of the Crime

As previously indicated, it will generally not be necessary to use force to effect the arrest of the embezzling bookkeeper, yet the use of force must be anticipated during the planning of any arrest operation. Surely anyone facing the loss of freedom may decide to resist, but most people will be able to rationalize between the consequences of arrest for minor or nonviolent crimes and violent crimes such as assaults, robberies, rapes, or homicides. You should always anticipate resistance during the arrest of someone being taken into custody for a violent crime. You must also consider whether or not your target used a weapon during the commission of the crime, in which case it is recommended that you assume that he/she will have a weapon on them or nearby.

10.2 Background

During the investigation of the crime, a full background investigation should have been conducted on the individual about to be apprehended. In addition to the behavior that was exhibited during the crime, the person's previous tendency toward violent behavior may have been learned by reviewing any prior arrest reports, interviews with relatives, neighbors, or associates, the use of drugs, and any medical, psychological, or psychiatric information you may become aware of.

10.3 Arrest Location

Since you know the identity and whereabouts of your suspect, you will not be relying on a chance encounter to make an arrest. Great care should be given to deciding on the location and time of the arrest. If you are concerned that your suspect may be armed or will otherwise resist arrest, you may wish to avoid locations where civilians are present. You may also wish to avoid places that may provide the defendant with additional weapons, such as an automobile repair shop, although arresting persons at their place of work can be beneficial since they may feel inhibited in exhibiting violent behavior in front of their peers.

10.4 Surprise and Immobilization

The element of surprise should be considered in every situation where the use of force is anticipated. The swiftness with which the apprehension is accomplished will go a long way toward eliminating resistance on the part of the defendant. In order to ensure safety to law enforcement personnel and defendants alike, all arrests should include the immediate immobilization of the subject. Your department's guidelines and procedures should be followed with respect to the use of force, yet it is never inappropriate to place the defendant in a position from which he/she is unable to inflict harm on you or others.

10.5 Equipment and Backup Personnel

Somehow Inspector Lestrade rarely needed assistance, other than the pointed logic of Sherlock Holmes, to convince defendants to submit to arrest. On the other hand, "Dirty" Harry Callahan's handcuffs never seemed to have seen the light of day; instead, his .44 magnum resulted in "morgue wagons" rather than "paddy wagons."

Your safety and the safety of those around you are of paramount importance and create the premise that allows you to use physical and sometimes deadly physical force. It is with safety in mind that you should ensure that the proper equipment and personnel are on hand to assist you in effecting the arrest. While it may be macho to put your shoulder to the door to knock it down, it is certainly not safe or practical to do so. If in order to effect the arrest you need to break into an area, it is highly recommended that you seek the assistance of people and equipment designed for the job. Communications equipment is also essential for all members of the arrest team.

10.6 Ingress/Egress

When planning an apprehension, all members of your team should be aware of the physical location, including all streets, entrances, exits, and the location of all rooms, furniture, staircases, etc., if the arrest will take place inside of a building.

10.7 Number of Potential Arrests

The number of persons to be apprehended at any given location will present special logistical and manpower requirements. Assignments regarding the apprehension and immobilization of each subject should be decided beforehand, making sure there are enough handcuffs available to individually secure each defendant rather than handcuffing them to each other.

10.8 Transportation of Prisoners

Prior to leaving for the arrest sight, you will need to arrange for sufficient transportation for the number of persons being arrested. It may be as simple as transporting one prisoner, rear-cuffed in the back of your vehicle, or you may need a prisoner van or paddy wagon to transport multiple prisoners. If you are forced to transport multiple prisoners together, they should be individually secured inside the vehicle to protect the safety of the officer who will be with them for the purpose of preventing collaboration among them.

You must also know where you are transporting them. Are all or some of them going back to the detective's office for interrogation, or are they going to the DA's office, a booking facility, or a combination of these places?

Testifying

11

As a law enforcement investigator you will inevitably be required to give testimony regarding your cases. You may be called to testify in both criminal and civil courts, as happened in the O.J. Simpson and Rodney King cases, and at the local, state, or federal level. Whether you are testifying at a civil deposition regarding a fatal automobile accident or before a judge and jury in a capital murder case, your obligation is the same: Be prepared, appear professional, and deliver clear, concise, and truthful answers to those questions that are appropriate.

11.1 Preparation

Preparation begins with the writing of the very first report. It may take a considerable amount of time, sometimes years, before a particular case will come to trial. It is quite possible that you will have investigated hundreds of other cases during the interim. There will be many similarities between investigations, including crimes that happen on the same streets, in the same bars, often with the same witnesses, and even sometimes with the same victims. Your ability to give professional testimony depends on your skill in preparing and maintaining accurate records.

You are not the only person that will need preparation before trial. The prosecutor assigned to the case has the ultimate responsibility to understand and present the facts, and in doing so the prosecutor must prepare the witnesses before trial. You are one of those witnesses. Before you meet with the prosecutor, you should review your entire investigative file, know where all of the evidence is located and make sure that it is available, and confirm the whereabouts of all witnesses if the prosecutor has not already done so or previously asked you to do it. You must be sure that your investigative file is complete and contains copies of all reports in chronological order, lab reports, evidence vouchers, and any documents, news stories, information, or reports from other departments, agencies, or other sources.

If the testimony you are about to give is before a trial court, you should review transcripts of any prior testimony you may have given in this case. This review could be the most important part of your pretrial preparation, since you can be sure that the defense attorney will have reviewed each and every word you have previously uttered under oath. It is the defense attorney's job to find and exploit any inconsistencies, in an effort to discredit you and the evidence that has been amassed against his or her client. It is your job to be consistently truthful throughout the entire process and avoid making mistakes.

11.2 Testimony as Public Speaking

Giving testimony at a trial is a unique form of public speaking. Some of the following public speaking tips from the Toastmasters International can be helpful to all investigators as well.

10 Tips for Successful Public Speaking

Feeling some nervousness before giving a speech is natural and healthy. It shows you care about doing well. But too much nervousness can be detrimental. Here's how you can control your nervousness and make effective, memorable presentations:

1. *Know the room.* Be familiar with the place in which you will speak. Arrive early, walk around the speaking area, and practice using the microphone and any visual aids.
2. *Know the audience.* Greet some of the audience as they arrive. It's easier to speak to a group of friends than to a group of strangers.
3. *Know your material.* If you're not familiar with your material or are uncomfortable with it, your nervousness will increase. Practice your speech and revise it if necessary.
4. *Relax.* Ease tension by doing exercises.
5. *Visualize yourself giving your speech.* Imagine yourself speaking, your voice loud, clear, and assured. When you visualize yourself as successful, you will be successful.
6. *Realize that people want you to succeed.* Audiences want you to be interesting, stimulating, informative, and entertaining. They don't want you to fail.

7. *Don't apologize.* If you mention your nervousness or apologize for any problems you think you have with your speech, you may be calling the audience's attention to something they hadn't noticed. Keep silent.

8. *Concentrate on the message — not the medium.* Focus your attention away from your own anxieties and outwardly toward your message and your audience. Your nervousness will dissipate.

9. *Turn nervousness into positive energy.* Harness your nervous energy and transform it into vitality and enthusiasm.

10. *Gain experience.* Experience builds confidence, which is the key to effective speaking. A Toastmasters club can provide the experience you need.*

Certainly not every point listed here can be taken literally with respect to testifying, yet they all contain certain aspects that are germane. For example, while you will not be able to "Greet some of the audience as they arrive," you will have an opportunity to get to know the judge and/or the jury during the time you are on the witness stand, and, more importantly, they will get the opportunity to know you as well. You will become familiar with the courtroom so that you know where judge, jury, prosecutor, defense counsel, and defendant are located. You, above all others, should now know the material you are to present. Relaxation is enhanced by thorough knowledge of the material. Visualization is a proven technique in speaking as well as in sports. Prior to hitting a golf ball, Tiger Woods can be seen taking practice swings while looking down the fairway. He is visualizing his next swing in much the same way that you can visualize yourself confidently answering questions on cross-examination. The judge, jury, and prosecutor all want you to succeed in your testimony so that they can evaluate your information and fulfill their judicial functions. Your failure on the stand is within the domain of the defense attorney. You should not appear apologetic or defensive while giving testimony; rather, you should portray yourself as a confident professional with an excellent command of the facts. Concentrate on the questions being asked of you, and formulate your response based on the facts. Do not ramble or provide information that was not asked for. Convert your nervous energy into alertness. Look forward to every opportunity to testify, since each occasion will be a learning experience that will add to your confidence.

* http://www.toastmasters.org/tips.asp

11.3 Making a First Impression

As the saying goes, "You will only have one chance to make a first impression." It is not necessary for you to wear expensive clothing, but looking anything less than neat and well groomed will have an adverse effect on the perception of professionalism you should strive to portray. A suit and tie for men and a business suit for women is highly recommended. If your testimony is going to span more than one day, try not to wear the same clothing more than once. Your hair should be neatly trimmed and combed, unless there is an appropriate reason, such as your being assigned to the investigation of narcotics cases. Five o'clock shadow should be avoided, and mustaches, beards, and sideburns should appear neat, and fingernails should be well manicured.

As you take the witness stand, you should attempt to make eye contact with the judge, and it is appropriate for you to acknowledge the judge by saying "Good morning, your Honor." You may also wish to look at the jurors and give them a brief smile and nod, as if to wish them a good day as well. Your ability to "break the ice" with the judge and jury cannot be underestimated.

You will be asked to take an oath prior to giving testimony. Your answer will help give that first impression you are looking to establish. While standing in the witness box, maintain a good posture, look directly in the eyes of the person administering the oath, and allow approximately one second to pass before you clearly and firmly say, "I do!"

11.4 Speaking to the Judge and Jury

Judges and Jurors will try to relate to witnesses during the course of the trial, but most witnesses will be fixated on the person asking them questions. A professional witness is one who can look at and listen to the person asking the question but speak to the only people in the courtroom that really matter: the judge and jurors. This is a difficult concept to master since most of us have been socialized since childhood to speak to and look at people with whom we are engaged in conversation. In the courtroom it is best to look at the prosecutor or defense counsel when he or she is asking the questions, but turn and face the jurors (or the judge in a nonjury trial) when you provide the answers. Since this can be very disconcerting to the person asking the questions, you should advise the prosecutor in advance of your intention to use this testimony style. If the defense counsel is made uncomfortable by this technique, he/she may become agitated and abrasive and may attempt to get you to change your style and look at him/her. You should never become argumentative on the witness stand; rather, you should simply address the judge directly and say that it is your intention to provide testimony to the jurors, or to the judge if no jury is present. If the judge directs you to look at the defense attorney when you answer, so be it, but you should continue to make eye contact with the jurors at every opportunity.

11.5 Pace of Testimony

The pace of the questions and answers is also very important, especially on cross-examination. It is a good habit to count to three or to use some other measure to allow time to elapse between the end of the question and your answer. Not only will this allow you the time formulate your answer, but it will provide the prosecutor with the opportunity to make an objection to inappropriate questions. If you rush to answer immediately, you may inadvertently provide an answer that may be objected to by the prosecutor and sustained by the judge, who will then instruct the jury to "disregard what you have heard." Can you envision the jury reviewing your testimony on a key issue and having the jury foreman stand up and say, "But the judge said we should disregard that answer!" There is a strong probability that not every juror can forget what he or she has heard. The best way to avoid this problem is to take your time before answering questions.

Your answers should be provided in a firm and clear voice and in sentences that are short and to the point. You will not be asked for your opinions unless you have been qualified as an expert in some particular area. You should not attempt to give your opinions or embark on long-winded explanations unless you are asked to do so. Most questions asked of you on cross-examination will best answered in short responses like "yes" or "no," "I don't know," or "I don't recall." Remember, don't become argumentative under cross-examination.

11.6 "Your Honor, May I Review My Reports?"

Even though you have reviewed the investigative file prior to discussing the case with the prosecutor, you should not rely on your memory alone. You will be able to bring your investigative file with you to the witness stand, and it is quite appropriate for you to ask the judge for permission to review your records prior to answering a question that you are not certain about. Do not guess at answers! Ask for permission to review your notes, take you time doing so, and then provide the appropriate answer in your own words rather than reading directly from the reports.

11.7 Demeanor

You should attempt to maintain a consistent demeanor while on the witness stand, regardless of whether the questions are being asked on direct or cross-examination. This is more difficult than it appears. The prosecutor has already prepared you to testify, and you will already be familiar with his/her questions. The defense attorney will have had the opportunity to review all of your reports and prior testimony and will have a list of questions designed to make you appear uncomfortable and less than professional. It is important to answer these questions with the same tone and pace as you answered the prosecutor's questions. Be prepared for questions that challenge your experience, your competency, and your actions or lack of actions. You may be asked questions regarding your department's investigative and arrest policies or generally accepted investigative procedures, such as safeguarding crime scenes. You may be asked questions that challenge your honesty and integrity, but your ability to remain unruffled will have an impact on the judge and jury. Again, maintain your pace and your composure, and allow sufficient time after the question is asked for the prosecutor to voice an objection.

Investigative Tools 12

A great many investigative tools have been developed to assist criminal investigators with their cases. Many of these tools are contained within one place: the forensic lab. Scientific tests can make unseen fingerprints, bodily fluids, filed-down serial numbers, and other hidden trace evidence miraculously appear. Others of these tests can match fabrics, tire tread marks, tool marks, etc. For further in-depth study in the field of forensics, the author recommends the following works: Dr. Henry C. Lee, *Crime Scene Handbook*; Stuart H. James and Jon J. Nordby, *Forensic Science*, 2nd ed.; and Vernon Geberth, *Practical Homicide Investigations*, 3rd ed. This chapter discusses the use of other tools and techniques not provided by the forensic lab.

12.1 Polygraph

The answer to the question of whether or not polygraph examinations are accurate in criminal investigations is yes and no. A properly administered polygraph examination in a case involving substantial criminal penalties will usually result in an accurate finding of truth or deception. A polygraph instrument is designed to measure changes in a person's respiration, blood pressure, and heartbeat, and the body's resistance to electricity by measuring the galvanic skin response, or GSR. The skin will conduct electricity much easier when it is moist from sweat. The test is designed to evoke psychological responses from the subject that in turn will produce physiological changes that can be measured by the polygraph instrument.

Unfortunately, a polygraph exam also depends on the training, skill, and experience of the polygraph examiner. A poorly prepared or administered polygraph examination will produce unreliable test results.

This theory behind the polygraph examination has its origin with primeval man and is commonly referred to as the "fight or flight" response.

Simply put, when a person perceives danger, the body automatically and subconsciously produces adrenaline, also known as epinephrine:

> **Epinephrine**: hormone important to the body's metabolism, also known as adrenaline. Epinephrine, a catecholamine, together with norepinephrine, is secreted principally by the medulla of the adrenal gland. Heightened secretion, caused perhaps by fear or anger, will result in increased heart rate and the hydrolysis of glycogen to glucose. This reaction, often called the "fight or flight" response, prepares the body for strenuous activity.[*]

The result of this excess sugar and oxygen is an increase in energy, strength, and alertness that is often referred to as an adrenaline rush. Most individuals have experienced this heightened state of alertness, which is usually accompanied by a dry mouth or sweaty palms, dilated pupils, and other notable physical changes. The result during a polygraph examination will be the recording by the polygraph instrument of the changes in the subject's breathing pattern, heart rate/blood pressure, and GSR.

It is not enough for the subject simply to demonstrate these physiological changes; rather, the changes must occur in a timely fashion to either a relevant question or a control question. Theoretically, the physiological changes will be more pronounced in response to questions that pose a greater threat. For the guilty person, the greater threat should be the question relating to his/her involvement in the crime. But what about the innocent person, won't he or she also react to that relevant question for fear of being wrongly accused? More than likely he/she will, which is why control questions that should be more threatening to an innocent person are provided as well. These control questions are intentionally designed to get the test subject to lie about them or to face the belief that the examiner will think that he/she has committed the crime in question. Neutral questions are also asked, from which baseline readings are obtained.

The following is a brief overview of a typical polygraph examination. Prior to administering the polygraph test, the examiner will interview the investigator to obtain a complete briefing. The polygraph examination will begin with the pretest interview of the subject, done in the same room where the test is to be administered, in full view of the polygraph instrument. The room and atmosphere should be nonthreatening (no jail cells, no handguns worn by the examiner, etc.), but a two-way mirror is appropriate. The examiner should begin to create a rapport with the subject, have him/her sign any release forms, authorizations, or Miranda waivers if necessary, and then in a

---

[*] *The Columbia Encyclopedia*, 6th ed., 2001.

general sense explain the workings of the scientific equipment known as the polygraph instrument.

It is recommended that all polygraph examinations be recorded, either on audiotape or audio-videotape. This can be done without the consent of the subject in states that require just one-party consent to recordings. In two-party states, the subject should be asked to sign a consent form.

The next stage of the test will be the subject interview. The subject should be allowed to tell the entire story, without interruption. If the subject's story wanders or pauses for long periods, the examiner should ask short, open-ended questions to get him/her back on track. The examiner will be listening for the subject to explain how he/she became involved in this situation, why the police think that he/she may be involved, what the subject actual thinks happened, who the suspect actual thinks committed the crime, and what the subjects alibis may be. If the subject has not provided this information during the initial part of this interview, the examiner should explore them with the subject once he/she has finished telling the story.

The examiner should then review his/her notes with the subject to elim-inate any areas of confusion. The examiner may then choose to leave the room, telling the subject that he/she is going to his/her office to compose the test questions, or he may just chose to stay in the examination room and ask the subject to remain silent while he/she constructs the test questions.

Once the test questions have been constructed, the examiner will review each question with the subject in advance, in the order in which they will be asked on the actual tests. The examiner will explain the "yes" or "no" answer format of the test and will have the subject answer each question beforehand. It is during this process that the attention of a deceptive person will be directed to the relevant questions and the truthful person's attention directed to the control questions. The examiner may have to readjust the control question to ensure that it is being answered falsely by either a truthful or a deceptive subject. The examiner will also explain that the test will be admin-istered at least twice but maybe more to ensure the scientific integrity of the process.

Once the test has been explained and the questions answered appropri-ately by the subject, the examiner will then ask the subject to be seated in the examination chair, and the equipment will be attached. The examiner will instruct the subject to sit very still during the examination, since any movements will be detected by the equipment and may make it necessary to conduct additional tests.

It is not uncommon for guilty subjects to make spontaneous confessions at any stage prior to the actual administration of the test. For some people the combination of visible scientific equipment and a scientific explanation of how the body reacts when a person attempts deception are sufficient to cause them to admit to their involvement, before a single question has been asked. If this occurs, the polygraph examiner should be allowed to continue with the interrogation process, including the issuance of Miranda warnings if not already obtained, so as to memorialize the confession.

Once the testing begins, the examiner will ask the exact questions that were posed to the subject prior to the test, speaking in a monotone, without special emphasis on any question. The timing of the questions will be evenly spaced, leaving enough time for the physiological reactions and recovery. After the first test, the examiner will turn off the instrument and instruct the subject to relax for a moment while the examiner reviews the chart. Prior to reactivating the instrument for the second test, the examiner will inform the subject that the first test was recorded without problem and that the second test is about to begin, or the examiner may tell the subject there was some problem with the recording of the first test due to excessive movement, coughing, etc., and let the subject know that at least one additional test will be required. The investigator may review the questions with the subject again but may change the order of the relevant questions on the second and any subsequent tests. This change in order will be told to the subject rather than it making it a surprise. There should be no surprise questions on a polygraph examination.

When all of the testing is over, the examiner will return to his/her office to analyze and score the results, telling the subject to remain in the room until he/she returns. It is advisable to have someone watch the subject through the two-way mirror at all times when the subject is alone in the testing room.

The examiner will review each chart for any physiological changes that may have occurred along the time continuum as they relate to the types of question asked. From these changes the examiner will develop a score for each chart and finally will inform the investigator if the charts indicate truthfulness or deception or are inconclusive. If deception is the finding, it is best to allow the examiner to confront the subject, conduct an interrogation, and seek a confession. If truthfulness is the finding, there is no need for the examiner to speak with the subject again and the subject can leave with the investigator. If the test is inconclusive, the examiner may wish to speak with the subject again and try to determine why. Drugs and alcohol consumption can affect polygraph results and produce inconclusive results. A confusing set of facts or different levels of the subject's involvement in a crime can produce inconclusive results. The examiner may try to clear up any confusion, conduct additional tests, or ask that the subject return on another day.

12.2 Voice Stress Analysis

The use of voice stress analysis by law enforcement agencies has grown dramatically in recent years, yet the controversy surrounding the validity of this technology continues to grow as well.

Unlike the scientific scrutiny that the polygraph has undergone throughout the years, most of the validity claims for accuracy for voice stress analysis appear to come from testimonials rather than scientific studies. The following conclusion is from a study conducted by the Department of Defense:

> A number of features of the voice have been reported to reflect psychological stress. If these claims were validated, this technology could have significant medical and deception detection applications. Unfortunately, the reports have been inconsistent, possibly due to failure to utilize robust stress paradigms supported by validated physiological and biochemical indices of stress. Using a well-characterized stressful interview model, we examined the capabilities of a commercial computer voice stress analyzer (CVSA), which is purported to measure "physiological microtremor," or frequency modulation, in the voice. Although a number of validated stress indices, including heart rate, blood pressure, plasma ACTH, and salivary cortisol, were all increased by the interview, no effect was seen in the CVSA data. Because of the potential medical value of a reliable voice stress analysis system, other available technologies assessing different voice features should be examined using this robust stress paradigm.
>
> This study was approved by the Human Subjects Research Review Board of the Office of the Surgeon General of the U.S. Army.[*]

The following quote is from the "Conclusions and Recommendations" of the State of Virginia's *Study of the Utility and Validity of Voice Stress Analyzers*:

> Because there have been no independent scientific studies conducted on the reliability of the computer voice analyzer to detect deception, the Board recommends to the Directory of the Department of Professional and Occupational Regulation that computer

---

[*] DoDPI Research Division Staff, J. L. Meyerhoff, G. A. Saviolakis, M. L. Koenig, & D. L. Yourick. *Physiological and biochemical measures of stress compared to voice stress analysis using the computer voice stress analyzer (CVSA).* January 2001, Report No. DoDPI98-R-0004. Department of Defense Polygraph Institute, Fort Jackson, SC 29207.

voice analyzer equipment should not be approved in Virginia at this time.""*

As with the polygraph, the theory of voice stress analysis is based on the psychological-physiological phenomenon of "fight or flight." When a person is under stress, micro-muscle tremors (MMT) occur in the muscles that make up the vocal tract, and these tremors are detectable through analysis of the individual's speech. The scientific instrument commonly referred to as a voice stress analyzer (VSA) measures the changes in MMT in a person's voice that occur as a result of answering a series of relevant, control, and neutral questions.

The VSA test is conducted in a similar fashion to that of the polygraph exam, with the VSA examiner first interviewing the investigator and then conducting a pretest interview with the subject. As with the polygraph, the validity of the scientific instrument is explained and stressed prior to administering the exam. Unlike the polygraph, the subject is not connected to the VSA instrument, and only one physiological reaction (MMT) will be measured.

It is not unusual for subjects to make spontaneous confessions prior to the start of the actual test. If that is the case, the VSA examiner should be allowed to continue with the interrogation, including Miranda warnings if the test subject did not previously sign a waiver.

After the test the examiner will review all of the charts and make a determination of truth or deception or inconclusive results.

Investigators must keep in mind that both the polygraph and the VSA are only tools to be used in the furtherance of an investigation. Neither of these techniques is recommended for use at the beginning of your investigation, but instead near the end, when a suspect has been identified, or at anytime when a witness is believed to be lying and all other avenues of investigation have been explored. The laws with respect to the introduction of these tests in criminal courts vary throughout the county, yet most courts will accept them as evidence on stipulation or consent from the opposing party.

12.3 Psychics

Unlike polygraph or voice stress analysis, psychics are not used by investigators to confront suspects or witnesses; rather, their purported clairvoyant ability is directed toward finding missing people, crime scenes, etc. Their

---

* Virginia Department of Professional and Occupational Regulation, *Study of the utility and validity of voice stress analyzers*, Adopted: November 17, 2003.

value as an investigative tool has been reviewed by the scientific community and law enforcement alike, with the results being that psychics provide little or no real facts that are suitable for investigative follow-up. Yet there are investigators who report successes in using psychics to assist them in certain cases.

It would require a belief in paranormal, mystical, or telepathic abilities for an investigator to allocate man-hours to follow up on the generally vague leads that are usually produced by psychics. This leap of faith is not usually found among investigators, who are trained to seek physical evidence that can be scientifically confirmed. This book does not advocate the use of psychics.

12.4 Criminal Profiling

Perhaps the greatest and best-known criminal profiler was the fictional detective Sherlock Holmes. His renowned powers of observation, combined with his skilled deductive reasoning and knowledge of psychology and psychiatry, provided for the most entertaining profiles of his adversaries.

Sadly there are few real-life equivalents of this legendary investigative icon. While the most widely known criminal profiling program in the world is the FBI's Behavioral Science Unit, their profiles can sometimes be misleading and threadbare, since they are generally based on statistical odds that the person who committed the crime at hand will have something in common with other criminals who have been arrested for similar crimes in the past. This type of thinking may have had its origins with Cesare Lombroso, a 19th century physician who believed criminals had certain inherited criminal instincts. "Lombroso's fame rests above all on his theory of the atavistic or born criminal, the individual whose physical structure possesses the degenerative traits that differentiate him from the normal, socially well-adjusted man."* While Lombroso's theories are generally discounted in modern criminology, to construct a criminal profile based mainly on the nature or the type of crime that has been committed, the type of weapon used, the location of the crime, etc., is really no different from Lombroso's original belief that criminals were born with certain physical traits, such as very long arms, beady eyes, and cleft palate.

When the general public hears the words *criminal profile,* they assume the profiler has used some mysterious combination of observation and psychological analysis to identify what the criminal looks like, what type of work he/she does, and his/her hobbies, marital status, and sexual preference, and by doing so provides a road map to the ultimate arrest. The reality at best

---

* Museo Criminalogico. http://www.museocriminologico.it/lombroso_1_uk.htm

seems to indicate that profiles are very useful in determining if there are relationships between different crimes, indicating a serial criminal. This is primarily done by an analytical review of all of the crime scene evidence, photographs, video, sketches, witness statements, etc., and comparing them to other, similar crimes.

According to Geberth, "Criminal personality profiling is usually productive in crimes in which an unknown subject has demonstrated some sort of psychopathology in his crime, for example: sadistic torture in sexual assaults, evisceration, postmortem slashing and cutting, motiveless fire-setting, lust and mutilation murders, ritualistic crimes, and rapes."[*]

Obviously, not all crime scenes are suited for personality profiling. Some scenes will be devoid of significant evidence of psychological deviance, and not all murderers become serial killers.

According to Dr. Maurice Godwin:

> The FBI has never caught a serial killer. Not a one. The profiles they turn out on serial killers are closer to Harris's [referring to Thomas Harris, author of *Silence of the Lambs*] fiction than scientific fact. They are based upon interviews conducted in 1978 with 36 convicted killers, out of which only 25 were actual serial killers. That FBI "study" has since been condemned as statistically and demographically invalid by one academic after another. But because that condemnation has come from inside the ivy-covered walls of academia, and the police culture refuses to allow a dissenting opinion, the media has ignored the Bureau's sleight-of-hand.[†]

In his book *Tracker, Hunting Down Serial Killers*, Dr. Godwin provides insight into just how far off the mark the FBI's profiles were on some of the most publicized serial or spree killer investigations, citing the Unabomber, Ted Kaczynski, and the D.C. Sniper as just two such examples.

While some criminal profilers may possess a combination of psychological education and law enforcement background, it appears there is no real basis for much of their conclusions. As Dr. Godwin points out when talking about the FBI's faulty profiles in two other notorious cases:

> In the Wallace case [Henry Lee Wallace, Charlotte, NC], and as we shall see in the case of the Baton Rouge Serial Killer, everyone

---

[*] Vernon J. Geberth, *Practical homicide Investigations: Tactics, procedures, and forensic techniques*, 3rd ed. (CRC Press, 1996), p. 711.
[†] Maurice Godwin and Fred Rosen, *Tracker, Hunting Down Serial Killers* (Thunders Mouth Press, 2005), p. 41.

but me profiled the offender as white. Perhaps that's because there is an inherent bias in the FBI profile to stay away from defining African Americans as serial criminals. Yes, about 16% of serial killers are African Americans, but in the FBI model it's as if African Americans don't exist at all.[*]

12.5 Deductive Profiling

Yet, profiling has many advocates and has produced good results in many cases. Brent E. Turvey, MS, the author of *Criminal Profiling: An Introduction to Behavioral Evidence Analysis*, 2nd ed., is an advocate of what he describes as "deductive profiling," as opposed to the "inductive profiling" that is utilized by the FBI. In his 1998 essay titled *Deductive Criminal Profiling: Comparing Applied Methodologies Between Inductive and Deductive Criminal Profiling Techniques*, Turvey suggests that using historical survey information that is "generalized from limited population samples, and not specifically related to any one case" whose "profiles are generalized and averaged from the limited data collected only from known, apprehended offenders" must be inherently inaccurate since it totally ignores "the most intelligent or skillful criminal populations: the criminals who are successful in continually avoiding detection by law enforcement."[†]

According to Turvey:

The data used to infer a deductive criminal profile for a particular criminal includes the following:

Forensic Evidence: A full equivocal forensic analysis must be performed before profiling can begin, to ensure the integrity of the behavior and the crime scene characteristics that are to be analyzed. Nothing can be assumed by the profiler.

Crime Scene Characteristics: Crime scene characteristics are determined from all forensic reports, all forensic analysis, and all forensic documentation which provides the nature of the interaction between the victim(s), the offender, and the location(s) of the offense during the occasion of a specific offense. In cases involving a related series of offenses, such as in serial rape, or serial

[*] Maurice Godwin and Fred Rosen, *Tracker, Hunting Down Serial Killers* (Thunders Mouth Press, 2005), p. 50.
[†] B. Turvey, Deductive criminal profiling: Comparing applied methodologies between inductive and deductive criminal profiling techniques, *Knowledge Solutions Library*, January 1998, Electronic Publication, http://www.corpus-delicti.com/Profiling_law.html

homicide, crime scene characteristics are determined individually and analyzed as they evolve, or fail to evolve, over time. An offender's crime scene characteristics, in a single offense or over multiple offenses, can lend themselves to inferences about offender motive, modus operandi, and the determination of crime scene signature.

Victimology: Victimology is the thorough study and analysis of victim characteristics. The characteristics of an individual offender's victim population of choice, in a single offense or over time, can lend themselves to deductive inferences about offender motive, modus operandi, and the determination of crime scene signature. In deductive profiling, almost as much time is spent profiling each victim as the offender responsible for the crime(s).*

Deductive criminal profiling appears to be another phrase for a complete and thorough examination of the facts. Long before the terms *profiling* and *forensics* became popular, detectives were sometimes able to determine if a criminal was right- or left-handed, short or tall, heavy or slight of build, strong or weak, male or female, light- or dark-haired, etc. This type of "profile" and examination of the facts should certainly be conducted in every serious investigation.

It is possible that the application of clinical psychology and psychiatry to the observable actions of certain criminal's actions at crime scenes may produce valuable insight into the type of individual that committed the crime. It is also quite possible that it will not help at all and that it may even lead investigators in the wrong direction.

12.6 Geographic Profiling

Dr. Maurice Godwin advocates "geographic profiling" as an investigative tool to be used in conjunction with other investigative techniques:

The technique employs a variety of methods, including distance to crime research, demographical analysis, environmental psychology, landscape analysis, geographical information systems, point pattern analysis, crime site residual analysis, and psychological criminal profiling. This process has both quantitative and qualitative (landscape analysis) dimensions to its application. Moreover, GPA seems to be a particularly effective method for the

* B. Turvey, Deductive criminal profiling.

needs of police investigators attempting to solve complex serial crimes. The technique examines the spatial data connected to a series of crime sites and in this study, more specifically, victims' body dump sites and point of fatal encounter sites.*

Profiling, whether criminal personality, behavioral analysis, or geographic, should be viewed as an additional tool available to investigators in certain situations. Yet the reliance on these profiles of potential types of suspects or groups (e.g., white males between 25 and 30), to the exclusion of other possibilities, can take investigators in the wrong direction. The author does not discourage the use of either criminal profiling as practiced by the FBI, behavioral evidence analysis as advocated by Turvey, or the geographic profiling of Godwin, but he does warn investigators not to rely on them to the exclusion of other suspects or other investigative leads.

The Role of Criminal Defense Investigators

13

To this point we have addressed criminal investigations from the law enforcement perspective, with the understanding that it is beneficial for both law enforcement and criminal defense investigators (CDIs) to know the correct methods of criminal investigation. Yet, for criminal defense investigators it is not enough just to know what the police do; they must develop investigative techniques to identify what the police did not do or what was done incorrectly. Law enforcement investigators will be best advised to take notice of the methods used by criminal defense investigators as well, for they are the mirrors by which your work will be evaluated by a jury.

13.1 Innocent Until Proven Guilty

The foundation of the criminal justice system in the United States is the concept that every criminal defendant is innocent until proven guilty. It is from this basic tenet that the criminal defense investigator derives his/her moral authority. Every person has the right to a fair trial. But what could be fair about a trial in which the police conducted the only investigation? The courts have recognized that the indigent are not only entitled to legal representation by an attorney, they are also entitled to an investigator. Legal Aid Societies or Public Defender's Offices employ professional investigators, and certain municipalities provide investigators through a "panel" of private investigators, such as those that have agreed to work on indigent cases with defense attorney's on the "18-B Panel" in New York (referring to County Law Article 18-B, which provides government payment to these private attorneys and investigators).

For those defendants who are not indigent, there are fee-based private investigators who specialize in criminal defense cases. As in other fields of private investigation, many CDIs are former law enforcement officers, while others come from all walks of life. Education, training, and experience are essential in developing the expertise required to be a successful CDI.

13.2 Initial Investigation

A criminal defense investigator will usually be retained or assigned after a defendant has been formally charged with a crime. This delay will generally guarantee that the CDI will not have been present during the processing of any crime scene or interview of any witness, be privy to the leads available to the police, or have been present at the time of arrest. From this perspective, a criminal defense investigation is much like an inning in baseball; the police were up first, now it's time for the defense.

In these cases the CDI has usually been either retained by the defense attorney or assigned in the case of a public defender's or legal aid matter. Therefore, the initial meeting should be with the defense attorney. The defense attorney should have already interviewed his/her client and may be in possession of police or other records. It is at this meeting that a full investigative plan should be developed so that both the CDI and the attorney are on the same page. Keep in mind that clients do not always fully confide in or tell the truth to their attorneys, yet there must be complete trust between the attorney and the CDI. That being said, the CDI must be aware of the possibility that the attorney may unwittingly offer him/her bad information that was originally provided by the client.

13.3 Protection of Information

Generally, but not always, when a criminal defense investigator is working for a defense attorney, the information possessed by the CDI is considered attorney work product and is protected from disclosure by the attorney–client privilege. This will not be the case in investigations in which a defense attorney has not been retained. No legal "privilege" exists between an investigator and his client. Anytime a CDI is retained directly by a client defendant, the client's family, or a nonattorney representative, the CDI should make the retaining party aware of this fact and suggest that an attorney be retained to afford the protection of the attorney–client privilege.

13.4 Police Records

Once the CDI has learned all he or she can from the attorney, attention must turn to the police records. It is imperative that the CDI have a thorough understanding of the forms and procedures used by the investigating agency, thereby allowing the CDI to know if there are any record types that should be in the file but aren't. If some types of records are missing, the attorney should be notified immediately so that they can be obtained ASAP through the discovery process. These records and forms can be 911 tapes or transcripts, incident, response, or complaint forms, evidence vouchers, follow-up investigation reports, photographs, diagrams, lab requests and results, witness statements or affidavits, a chronological log of police and emergency personnel arriving and leaving the scene, correspondence from local or district commanders to the hierarchy of the department detailing unusual occurrences, and other records that may vary, depending on the investigative and administrative protocols of the local law enforcement agency. Additionally, any print media, TV video, and transcribed radio station reports relating to the incident should be obtained as well.

Some attorneys would rather have their own paralegals review these records, but the CDI must make the attorney aware that a paralegal will rarely possess the knowledge to properly assess the material, know what types of material should have been produced, or have the ability to "read between the lines." Furthermore, it will not be the paralegal who will be conducting the follow-up investigation and interviews, for which purpose an in-depth knowledge of all that is known about the case is imperative.

It is highly unlikely that the defense attorney will have received all of the potential discovery materials, media reports, and additional relevant materials prior to the retention of the CDI, yet the CDI should thoroughly review and analyze any materials that are available prior to the first meeting between the CDI and the client defendant.

13.5 Background Investigation of Defendant Client

There may be many background investigations for the CDI to conduct during this investigation, but none is more important than the one that must be conducted on the defendant client. It would be advantageous for the CDI to complete as much of this investigation as possible prior to the first meeting with the client. It is essential that the defense team be aware of the total criminal background of the client, the client's education and work history, the relationship between the client, the victim, and any witnesses, the client's medical history, and the history of drug or alcohol usage, treatment, or dependency.

13.6 Interviewing Defendant Clients

The first meeting with the client defendant should not be a surprise visit; rather, it should be arranged by the defense attorney in advance. It would be best for this meeting to be between the client and the CDI alone, rather than in the company of the attorney or his paralegal.

Defendant clients will not fit any one mold. Some may be CEOs of Fortune 500 companies, while others may be homeless, yet the CDI must develop the ability to relate to individuals anywhere along this spectrum. During this first meeting the CDI should attempt to create a rapport with the client and to assure the client that the CDI is "on his/her side." The CDI should speak in a proper manner and refrain from using slang or street vernacular until such time as the client does so.

The CDI should not assume that the defense attorney has explained the CDI's function, nor should the assumption be made that the client understands the criminal justice system. The CDI should take the time to explain that his/her job is to conduct a complete and thorough investigation of the incident, to review and examine all of the police actions and records, to interview all witnesses, including those not known to the police, to gather additional evidence, and to assist the defense attorney up to and including a trial.

It is at this point that the CDI should let the client know that the client's guilt or innocence will have no effect on how hard the CDI will work on the case; rather, the CDI is concerned with the protection of the client's constitutional right to a fair trial. Never assume that the client has told the truth, or the entire truth, to the defense attorney, and never assume they will tell it to you either. Nevertheless, the CDI should make every effort to convince the client that by not confiding the truth to the CDI and the defense attorney, the client is hurting rather than helping his/her chances.

Prior to the crime interview itself, the CDI will need to review the personal history of the client by obtaining a complete pedigree, beginning with the obvious — full name, DOB, SSN, height, weight, tattoos, scars, and birthmarks — and continuing through such areas as previous arrests, entire employment history, social services history, entire education history, including all schools attended, medical history, all relatives, all friends, all enemies, driving history, vehicles owned, hobbies, etc.

At the beginning of the crime interview it is essential that the CDI make a further attempt to gain the confidence of the client while pointing out the obvious problems involved in defending a client who is not telling the whole truth to the defense attorney and CDI. During this preliminary stage and continuing through the end of the interview the CDI should be observing the mental capacity, attitude, and body language of the client.

Once the CDI begins the crime interview it would be appropriate to review the basic facts of the crime, the police investigation, and the arrest circumstances with the client, because they are currently known to the CDI. The client should then be asked to provide his/her own version of all of the events leading up to and including the arrest. The client should be allowed to proceed at his/her own pace so long as he/she doesn't wander too far afield or get bogged down. The CDI should listen attentively to the narration, taking quick notes and paying particular attention to any details that vary from the known police investigation. Once the client is finished with the narration, the CDI should review the client's story with him/her to see if there are any misunderstandings between the CDI and the client. Once the client's version is agreed on, the CDI can begin to ask clarifying questions to ensure that all of the "who, what, why, when, where, and how" questions are fully addressed.

The CDI should then begin to address any discrepancies between the client and police versions. Are the time sequences the same? Are the witnesses the same? Does the client know the victim? If yes, how and for how long? Was the client at the crime scene? If so, did the client have permission or authority to be there? Had the client and/or the victim been using drugs or alcohol? If a weapon was used, did the client possess such a weapon? Does the client know if he/she has been placed at the crime scene by witnesses or by any forensic evidence? How did the police become aware of the client as a suspect? Did the police interview the client before the arrest? If so, where and how did this happen? Was the client free to leave at any time? If not, was he/she advised of his/her Miranda rights prior to questioning by the police? Did the client make any statements, oral, written, or video- or audiotaped? If so, what did the client say? Did the police seize anything from the client's person, residence, place of employment, etc?

If the CDI has been unable to clear up any major discrepancies, he/she should make one last effort to do so prior to leaving. The client should once again be reminded that neither the CDI nor the defense attorney would be able to provide adequate representation unless the client is fully truthful.

Once the initial client interview is completed, the CDI should either meet with or, at a minimum, speak to the defense attorney as soon after the interview as possible. The CDI should provide a layperson's assessment of the client's mental abilities, e.g., was he/she able to understand the nature of the crime he/she is charged with, did he/she understand the potential criminal penalties, will he/she be able to assist in his/her own defense, did he/she appear to be honest or was he/she lying about his/her participation, did he/she possess knowledge of the crime that only the perpetrator would have? Factually, the CDI can provide the defense attorney with any information that was learned that would contradict the police investigation, such as potential perpetrators, additional witnesses, client alibis, and inconsistent timelines.

13.7 Follow-Up Investigation

After a thorough review of the police investigation and the initial interview of the client, the CDI should be in a position to plan the remaining investigation. The CDI should make a list and prepare a file or folder for the victim, the client, and all known witnesses, some of whom may not be known to the police. A complete background investigation should be conducted for all witnesses, including their relationships to the victim, the defendant client, and each other. The CDI should look to the defense attorney to prepare subpoenas for any background materials that may not be public records.

Timelines should be constructed from the police records and from the information obtained from the client. These timelines may change as new information becomes available, but initially they will give the CDI a good perspective.

13.8 Crime Scene

Prior to interviewing the witnesses, the CDI should make a trip to the crime scene(s), bringing along copies of any police crime scene photos, sketches, etc. It is highly unlikely that the crime scene will still be secure by the time the CDI arrives, but the photos and diagrams will aid the CDI in evaluating the scene. It is preferable to visit the crime scene at about the same time of the day that the actual crime was committed so that it can be viewed under similar circumstances, as well as locating canvass witnesses who may be at or near the location at the same time every day. Keep in mind that such issues as seasonal weather variations (snow, heat, etc.) and time changes (e.g., EDT vs. EST) may have an effect on the scene and the availability of witnesses.

Once at the crime scene, the CDI should take photographs and video of the entire area, including all areas of ingress and egress, all windows and doors, stairways, etc. In cases where forced entry or unknown means of entry is an issue, the photographs should include close-ups of all door locks, doorframes, window locks, and window frames to document any tool marks.

The CDI should then prepare a diagram of the crime scene, including exact measurements, which can then be compared to the diagrams and measurements taken by the police. Particular attention should be paid to the vantage points claimed by victims and witnesses, to verify that they could have seen what they claimed to have seen and that their locations within the scene are accurately reflected on the police diagrams. The timelines should also be considered in the context of the crime scene, to determine if it was possible for certain events to have occurred within the allotted time frame.

In the event that the CDI observes any physical evidence at the scene that has not been previously collected, the evidence should be documented photographically or by videotape without being disturbed. The CDI should then contact the defense attorney for instructions regarding the disposition of the evidence, which may include notifying the police and safeguarding it until their arrival, bringing the evidence to an independent lab, bringing it directly to the police, obtaining a secure storage facility, etc. If the CDI is directed to collect the evidence, it should be collected in accordance with the accepted crime scene procedures previously discussed in this book. To minimize allegations that the CDI has "planted" the evidence at the scene, it is always advisable that the CDI be accompanied to the crime scene by another person, be it the defense counsel, a paralegal, or another CDI.

Since all crime scenes will be different, it is important for the CDI to evaluate each scene on its own merits and to attempt to learn everything possible about it prior to, during, and after the crime. This can include determining such things as (1) prior crimes committed at the location, (2) ownership of the location, (3) building code violations, (4) civil lawsuits based on the location, (5) street light and traffic light outages and sequences, (6) surveillance cameras recording the area (e.g., traffic control, parking lots, retail stores), (7) power outages, (8) system failures, such as elevator outages, (9) delivery schedules (e.g., fuel oil, building supplies), and (10) employee work schedules and routines.

13.9 Investigative Canvass

Once the CDI has finished with the physical crime scene(s), a complete and thorough witness canvass should be conducted, including the reinterview of all persons who provided information to the police. In addition to asking about their observations at the time of the crime, the CDI should be interested in determining if there had been any suspicious activity in the area prior to the crime and if it had been reported to the police. Additionally, it is likely that people in the area have been discussing this crime since the day of occurrence and the CDI may be able to learn about additional people who claimed to have information about it.

Regarding the observations of people identified in the police reports, the CDI should pay particular attention to any differences between what the person claims to have told the police and what appears in the police reports. Unless the person was a key witness, it is unlikely that a signed statement was obtained from them; rather, the police investigator may have recorded the general information in a notepad and used the notes and personal memory to prepare a formal report at a later date.

Particular attention should be paid to anyone who claims to have given information to the police but whose name does not appear in the police reports. The police investigation reports should include the information provided to them by everyone, and it is their responsibility to verify or disprove it. It is inappropriate for police investigators to intentionally omit information that may be exculpatory or that does not fit their theory, nor can they provide the prosecution with a surprise witness whose identity has been known all along.

Once all potential witnesses have been canvassed, it is time for the CDI to meet with the defense attorney, if one has been retained, or with the client if no attorney is involved. Good communication is essential for a good investigative plan. The investigator should fully review what has been learned, highlighting any discrepancies with the police investigation. The CDI may also learn about new information or records that have come to the attention of the attorney or defendant client.

The next phase of the investigation should be planned with the defense attorney, including a second interview with the defendant client, to clear up any areas of confusion and address both incriminating and exculpatory evidence. This meeting may influence a guilty client to reevaluate his/her chances of conviction, or it may stiffen the resolve of an innocent client to proceed to trial. This second interview of the defendant client will also allow the CDI to obtain additional information regarding the witnesses and any other information regarding the evidence.

13.10 Witness Interviews

The decision as to whether or not to take recorded or sworn statements from witnesses should be made by the defense attorney prior to the beginning of witness interviews, and to the extent possible the background investigation should be completed prior to the initial interview of the witness.

Not all witnesses are "eye witnesses" to the crime; rather, they can be anyone who can offer testimony at a trial. Witnesses can include police, firefighters, emergency medical technicians, and other fact witnesses, such as a bartender who can say that the victim left the bar at a particular time or a neighbor who saw the defendant enter the crime scene apartment at a particular time, predicate witnesses who may be called on to introduce official records, alibi witnesses, character witnesses, and expert witnesses who may be called on to give an opinion, or an eyewitness who alleges he saw the defendant pull out a gun from his waistband and shoot the victim in the chest.

There is no reason for CDI's to conduct interviews of predicate or expert witnesses, although background interviews of expert witnesses, including the discovery of prior testimony in similar cases, should be conducted.

Most police departments have rules and regulations that prohibit the disclosure of any information concerning cases that are pending prosecution. It is highly unlikely that police officers or detectives will consent to a voluntary interview, yet the possibility is not out of the question and should be pursued when deemed necessary. Firefighters and paramedics often have these same restrictions placed on them by their departments, especially when questions concern the release of any of the victim's personal medical information.

A key to interviewing witnesses is preparation. As already noted, the CDI should have conducted extensive background investigations of all known witnesses prior to conducting interviews. Additionally, the CDI should now be totally familiar with all of the available police records, have complete knowledge of the crime scene, and possess the information obtained from the client defendant and any other witness that has previously been interviewed by the CDI.

Prior to interviewing a witness, the CDI should prepare a general outline plan taking into consideration any previous statements given to the police. If the person is an eyewitness, the CDI should also plan on addressing timeline and crime scene issues, such as vantage points and the physical layout of the scene.

As in any other interview situation, the CDI must try to establish a rapport with the witness. It is appropriate for the CDI to use street language or vernacular once the witness has done so, thereby adjusting to the habits and mental traits of the witness.

The witness should be informed of the reason for the interview and who the CDI represents. If taking a recorded statement, the CDI should place a heading on the tape identifying the CDI, the date, time, and place of the interview, the case name, the identity of the witness, and identities of all other persons that are present. The witness should be asked to identify him-/herself by stating his/her full name, DOB, SSN, and address and providing his/her consent to the recording of the interview. If the CDI is also a notary, or if there is a notary present during the interview, an oath should be sworn to or affirmed by the witness to indicate that the information he/she is about to give is truthful. In situations where the witness's statement is written out rather than tape recorded, the same header information should be written in the introductory section of the statement, and the notarized oath should be written at the end of the statement, just above the signature of the witness.

The importance of complete pedigree information cannot be overstated. The CDI should make every effort to obtain as much information about the witness's personal life as possible, without becoming overly intrusive. Many witnesses will have transient or nomadic lifestyles, and locating them at the time of trial can sometimes become a full investigation unto itself. Every friend, relative, employer, etc., can become invaluable at a later date.

It is appropriate for the CDI to provide a brief description of the crime to the witness, to place the interview in the proper context. Once the CDI is comfortable that the witness has a clear understanding of the incident in question, the CDI should begin with an open-ended question designed to get the witness talking, such as, "Mr. Jones, I'm sure that you have gone over this incident in your mind a thousand times and I wish I could look into your mind and see what you saw. Do you think you can tell me everything that happened so that I can see it just as if I were watching a movie?" The aim is to get the witness to be as descriptive as possible as he/she provides a narration of the events. Once the witness begins talking, the CDI should take the role of active listener, taking only short notes when necessary and not interrupting the witness unless the witness begins to wander from the issues. Again, only open-ended questions should be used to get the witness back on track.

Once the witness has finished the narration, the CDI should momentarily review the notes just taken, checking to see whether or not the "who, what, why, where, when, and how" issues have been answered and paying particular attention to any discrepancies with previously obtained information. The CDI should then repeat the witness's version of the information to the witness, allowing the witness to correct any misunderstandings. It is sometimes a good technique for CDI to intentionally mistake a fact provided by the witness, affording the witness the opportunity to correct the CDI, thereby ensuring that the witness is actually paying attention.

Once this review is completed, the CDI can begin to ask direct questions based on the known facts of the case, e.g., differences between the current statement and the witness's prior statement to the police; how many interviews the witness has given and to whom; timeline and crime scene issues; description of the offender; any interaction between victim/offender/witnesses; weather; lighting; motive; relationships between victim/defendant/witnesses; witness background information, including physical health and capabilities (eyesight, hearing, mental impairment, etc.); drug and alcohol history; education; employment; etc.

If the decision has been made to record the interview or statement of an adversarial witness, the CDI should pay particular attention to matters that affect the witness's credibility or motives and to highlight any discrepancies between the current statement and the prior one given to the police or that is contradicted by other witnesses to the benefit of the defendant client.

The CDI should also observe the physical and emotional reactions of the witness so as to provide the defense attorney with an assessment of this individual as a trial witness. This assessment should include the CDI's appraisal of any ulterior motives of the witness, e.g., jealousy, rivalry, cover-up for themselves or another party.

The result of each witness interview should be reported to the defense attorney as soon after the interview as possible. Remember, good communication is essential for a good investigative plan. These reports can be verbal or written and can include the CDI's assessment of the facts and the witness. Once all witnesses have been interviewed, the CDI can again evaluate the police investigation, timelines, crime scene, and witnesses.

13.11 Report Writing

It is best to prepare written reports while the information is fresh in mind. Even the best note taker will lose valuable information and insight as time goes by. The CDI should not wait until the entire investigation is completed to prepare one overall report; rather, a series of timely, well-organized reports is encouraged.

Writing styles and abilities will vary greatly between individuals, yet at a minimum all reports should contain the identity of the person to whom the report is being submitted, the identity of the person submitting the report, the *caption* information, e.g., The People of the State of New York vs. John Doe, and the court docket number, the date of the report, and the subject of the report.

In order to make the reports user friendly, the writer may consider limiting each report to only one subject. That way, the reader will not have to search through a lengthy report to find one particular piece of information, such as an interview of a witness. For example:

SUBJECT: INTERVIEW EYEWITNESS JOHN SMITH:

On December 6, 2004, I met with witness John Smith at his residence, 1010 Prairie Dog Circle, Taos, NM. Mr. Smith is a white male, DOB 12/12/57, SSN 111-11-1111, and is employed at the Taco Bell located at 15 Chirping Dove Lane. Mr. Smith is approximately 6'3", 225 pounds, athletic in appearance, clean-shaven, short brown hair, and possessing average intelligence. Mr. Smith was cooperative and had good recall of this incident. He provided me with the following information....

If the interview of John Smith is the only topic being covered in this report, the reader will easily be able to find this information at a later date.

In the event that the writer wishes to combine multiple issues within one report (e.g., crime scene inspection, canvass, records obtained from DMV, interview eyewitness John Smith), the writer should clearly start the new subject by capitalizing it prior to the new paragraph. For example:

CRIME SCENE INSPECTION:

On December 3, 2004, I visited the crime scene, located at 2024 Tuscon Way, Taos, NM, apartment 3-B, a yellow two-story multiple dwelling....

CANVASS:

While at the crime scene I conducted a canvass of the following apartments within 2024 Tuscon Way:

Apt. 3-A: Mr. Walter Jones indicated that he was at home in his bedroom at approximately 10:30 P.M. on October 15, 2004, when he heard a male and female arguing loudly....

Apt. 3-C: Mrs. Maria Mendez indicated that at about 10:35 P.M. on October 15, 2004, she was looking out of her bedroom window when she heard a woman screaming from the apartment above hers, and several minutes later she observed a white male running toward a blue Ford Mustang, registration #....

OBTAINED DMV RECORDS:

On December 4, 2004, I traveled to the Arizona Department of Motor Vehicles and obtained the registrant and title documents for....

INTERVIEW EYEWITNESS JOHN SMITH:

On December 6, 2004, I met with witness John Smith at his residence, 1010 Prairie Dog Circle, Taos, NM. Mr. Smith is a white male, DOB 12/12/57, SSN 111-11-1111, and is employed at the

Taco Bell located at 15 Chirping Dove Lane. Mr. Smith is approximately 6'3", 225 pounds, athletic in appearance, clean-shaven, short brown hair, and possessing average intelligence. Mr. Smith was cooperative and had good recall of this incident. He provided me with the following information….

Reports containing multiple issues can be quite lengthy, but by clearly organizing the subjects beforehand, the writer will make it easier for the client to locate information he/she is looking for within the report without having to reread the entire report each time the information is needed.

There is no one best method for writing investigative reports, yet the CDI must understand that the report will be reviewed by the defense attorney and client, at a minimum, and should provide them with an important tool for the defense of the case. It will also provide a reflection of the quality of work that the CDI has produced. If the report is poorly written, contains misspelled words or grammatical errors, or is disorganized, the impression left with the reader will be negative. On the other hand, every defense attorney wishes to work with investigators who are organized and methodical and who produce a quality work product.

13.12 Trial Preparation

No one is more uniquely qualified to assist the defense attorney in the preparation for trial than the CDI. This fact should be stressed to your attorney clients at every opportunity, regardless of how many paralegals are working for the firm. As the CDI you should have become familiar with all of the witnesses, have intimate knowledge of the crime scene, know the strong points and weaknesses of the prosecution's case, be familiar with all of the evidence, have a complete understanding of police procedures, and have the ability to locate and produce the witnesses your client needs at trial.

13.13 Testimony

Unless you have been retained on appeal, your final involvement in the case as the CDI will likely end with the conclusion of the trial. It is not unusual for CDI's to testify at trial regarding certain aspects of their investigation. Perhaps you have discovered a previously missed piece of physical evidence or taken a key photograph or obtained a crucial recorded statement from someone who is now recanting or who perhaps has died or disappeared. Your ability to provide professional testimony is crucial and may have a dramatic effect on your client's future.

13.14 Appeals

If a defendant is convicted after a trial, he may consider filing an appeal to the next higher court. In general appeals can be made not simply because the defendant thinks the conviction was unjust, but because some significant legal error was allowed to go uncorrected during the trial. Appeals courts will not generally hear any new testimony, look at new evidence, or conduct a new trial; rather, the defendant's claim can only relate to things that have been recorded in the trial record. Some states, such as New York, do have mechanisms to allow for the introduction of facts that do not appear in the record of trial.

> No issue that does not appear on the record of the proceedings below may be raised on direct appeal to the appellate court. Section 440.10 of the Criminal Procedure Law, however, provides that, in certain circumstances, off-the-record issues may be raised by a motion to vacate a judgment made by the trial judge. Included among the grounds for such a motion are improper and prejudicial conduct not appearing in the record which would have resulted in reversal on appeal if it had appeared on the record, and the discovery of the new evidence that could not have been produced at the time of the trial which makes it possible that, had it been produced, it would have resulted in a more favorable verdict.[*]

Very few appeals are successful, and fewer still require the retention of a CDI. The most successful appeals cases are those that involve capital murder convictions. The success rate of appeals in death cases is probably not because prosecutors make more errors in these cases. Quite to the contrary, it is usually the best and most experienced prosecutors in their respective offices who handle death penalty cases. It does, however, appear that appellate courts grant more leeway to convicted defendants whose lives are on the line.

In the year 2000, in an analysis titled "The meaning of capital appeals: A rejoinder to Liebman, Fagan, and West," Barry Latzner, a professor, and James N. G. Cauthen, an assistant professor in the Department of Government at John Jay College of Criminal Justice, wrote the following in their review of a study titled "A Broken System: Error Rates In Capital Cases, 1973–1995," published by Professor James S. Liebman of the Columbia Law School:

---

[*] http://www.legal-aid.org/SupportDocumentIndex.htm?docid=5&catid=34

In death cases, errors ordinarily considered harmless are treated more seriously because the defendant's life is on the line. This lowered threshold for capital trial reversals is a virtual mandate of the Supreme Court. It does not mean, as Liebman, Fagan, and West suggest, that more and more serious errors occur in capital cases; it means simply that the ground rules of review are different and the scrutiny more intensive. The sentencing phase of capital trials, unique to death penalty cases, offers particularly fertile soil for findings of reversible error. As we have demonstrated, it is the source of 61% of all reversible error rulings[*]

Usually, the attorney who has undertaken the appeal will review the court transcripts for procedural and legal errors and any evidence that may be in question. Some of the issues on appeal can include allegations of faulty eyewitness identifications, illegally obtained confessions or evidence, previously unavailable DNA evidence, etc.

In the rare case that you are retained to assist in the investigation on an appeal, it will likely be in a death case. Since it appears that the courts may give more consideration to claims of new evidence, witnesses, DNA, and other information that was not presented at the original trial, a full reinvestigation may be requested by the defense counsel. This time, not only will you need to review all of the police investigation, you will also need to review all of the investigation that may have been conducted by previous CDI's. Each and every document associated with the case, whether or not they were presented at trial, should be reviewed again. The defendant client and all witnesses should be reinterviewed, the crime scene revisited, and all of the investigative procedures previously described redone.

Successful investigations on appeal cases are not measured by the final outcome of the appeal but, rather, by the evaluation of your work by the attorney client. Your knowledge of how to conduct a systematic examination of the facts will only serve to enhance your reputation as a professional investigator.

[*] http://www.lib.jjay.cuny.edu/docs/latzer_843.pdf

Index